A
THEOLOGICAL
MISCELLANY

T. J. McTAVISH

MJF BOOKS
NEW YORK

Published by MJF Books
Fine Communications
322 Eighth Avenue
New York, NY 10001

A Theological Miscellany
LC Control Number 2005935797
ISBN-13: 978-1-56731-753-4
ISBN-10: 1-56731-753-7

PREFACE

What you're holding is more than just a book. It's a labor of love. It's blood, sweat, and tears. It's the sum total of the knowledge I've been endowed with by the One who's seen fit to . . . uh, endow me. It's gold among the dross of other books. It's a shining testament to . . .

Okay, maybe it *is* just a book. But it's an extraordinarily unique one. In fact, it may very well save you a great deal of embarrassment. How many times have you been at a swanky dinner party when the conversation has turned to the popes who have served the shortest terms, or the five points of Calvinism, or famous bald men in the Bible, only to slink down into your chair in horror, realizing that you had nothing intelligent to add to the conversation? You didn't even know there were *three* points of Calvinism, much less *five*.

Well, be embarrassed no longer! Dive deeply into these pages . . . or skim the surface if you're afraid to commit. You'll come away amazed at your new-found sense of assurance in future theological conversations, your grasp of deep philosophical and biblical truths, and your annoyance at having wasted precious hours here while you could have been watching *Gilligan's Island* reruns.

Best wishes,
T. J. McTavish
November 2004

Thou art beside thyself;
much learning doth make thee mad.

—*Acts 26:24* (KJV)

❊ THE "FATHERS OF THE CHURCH" ❊

The term *Fathers of the Church* refers to the writings from the early Christian centuries by theologians, preachers, popes, and others. To be regarded as a Father, one must have orthodox doctrine; but this does not exclude all doctrinal error. An occasional material heresy can be found even in the greater lights among the Fathers.

Greek Fathers
Justin Martyr (100–165)
Athenagoras of Athens (late second century)
Irenaeus of Gaul (140–202)
Clement of Alexandria (150–215)
Hippolytus of Rome (170–236)
Origen of Alexandria (185–254)
Eusebius of Caesarea (263–340)
Cyril of Jerusalem (315–386)
Basil the Great (330–379)
Gregory of Nazianzus (329–389)
Gregory of Nyssa (330–395)
Theodore of Mopsuestia (350–428)
John Chrysostom (344–407)
Cyril of Alexandria (died 444)
John of Damascus (675–749)

Latin Fathers
Tertullian (160–220)
Cyprian of Carthage (died 258)
Lactantius (250–317)
Athanasius (297-373)
Hilary of Poitiers (315–367)
Ambrose of Milan (339–397)
Jerome (342–420)
Augustine of Hippo (354–430)
Prosper of Aquitaine (390–463)
Pope Gregory I "the Great" (540–604)

❊ THE PSALMS OF PENITENCE ❊

"Enter not into judgment with thy servant; for no man living is righteous before thee" (Ps. 143:2). This is the mood of seven of the Psalms, traditionally called the *Penitential Psalms*. In liturgical churches these psalms are often used on Ash Wednesday or during Lent. They are Psalms 6, 32, 38, 51, 102, 130, and 143.

❊ THE NATIONAL ASSOCIATION OF EVANGELICALS' ❊ STATEMENT OF FAITH

The National Association of Evangelicals exists "to extend the kingdom of God through a fellowship of member denominations, churches, organizations, and individuals, demonstrating the unity of the body of Christ by standing for biblical truth, speaking with a representative voice, and serving the evangelical community through united action, cooperative ministry, and strategic planning."
To that end, the organization embraces this statement of faith:

> We believe the Bible to be the inspired, the only infallible, authoritative Word of God.
>
> We believe that there is one God, eternally existent in three persons: Father, Son and Holy Spirit.
>
> We believe in the deity of our Lord Jesus Christ, in His virgin birth, in His sinless life, in His miracles, in His vicarious and atoning death through His shed blood, in His bodily resurrection, in His ascension to the right hand of the Father, and in His personal return in power and glory.
>
> We believe that for the salvation of lost and sinful people, regeneration by the Holy Spirit is absolutely essential.
>
> We believe in the present ministry of the Holy Spirit by whose indwelling the Christian is enabled to live a godly life.
>
> We believe in the resurrection of both the saved and the lost; they that are saved unto the resurrection of life and they that are lost unto the resurrection of damnation.
>
> We believe in the spiritual unity of believers in our Lord Jesus Christ.

❊ THREE POPES ARE TWO TOO MANY ❊

Occasionally in the history of the Roman Catholic Church, rivals have claimed the title of bishop of Rome or Supreme Pontiff. Some twenty-five *antipopes*, as they are styled, have been officially counted, and even in the twentieth century tiny splinter groups formed around someone claiming the title of pope. From 1309–1377, the popes were exiled in Avignon, France. From 1378–1417, a period known as the Great Schism,* there were both a pope in Rome and an antipope in Avignon, and later a third pope in Pisa. John XXIII, of the Pisa line, convened the Council of Constance (1414–1418), hoping to be declared the sole pope, eliminating the other two, Gregory XII and Benedict XIII. The council, however, deposed him and Benedict, and Gregory resigned. In 1417, Oddo Colonna was elected pope as Martin V, ending the period of "two popes too many."
    *The term *Great Schism* is also applied to the split between the Eastern and Western Churches in 1054.

❧ THE BIRTH OF JESUS AND THE MILLENNIUM ❧

According to Matthew, Jesus was born during the reign of Herod, who ruled Judea under the Romans. Herod died around April 1 in what we know as 4 BC. The Magi spoke with Herod before finding the child Jesus (Matt. 2:1–8). However, Herod was seriously ill during his last years, and he was in no condition to receive unfamiliar visitors; he stayed in Jericho part of the time and died there. The visit of the Magi, then, would have occurred earlier. Since their trip, from wherever they started, would have taken them some time before they reached the place where they found Jesus, a date of 4 BC for his birth is probably too late. Sometime in 6 BC might be more likely.

The third millennium would have started with the beginning of the 2001st year after the birth of Jesus. Starting with 6 BC, the 2001st year would have begun in 1995 (there is no year zero). When the year 2000 began, we would already have been in the third millennium for five years.

❧ THE CONSTRUCTION OF JEHOVAH ❧

As one philosopher quipped, "God made himself out of nothing." But we're talking about the *name* Jehovah, familiar for centuries as God's personal name. It never existed in biblical times, however. It came about this way.

The Hebrew alphabet includes only twenty-two letters standing for consonants. Vowels in Hebrew manuscripts are indicated by signs, called *points* by scholars, placed with the letters. Pious Jews didn't want to pronounce the holy name of God, written YHWH (Yahweh), so they substituted the word *Adonai* (Lord). Eventually, scribes started putting the vowel points for Adonai with the letters for YHWH so readers would remember not to pronounce the divine name. In the late Middle Ages, scholars who didn't understand this practice came up with the hybrid form Jehovah (J is pronounced like Y, as in German and other languages).

❧ CALENDARS: EAST MEETS WEST ❧

Why do your Greek Orthodox friends usually celebrate Easter a week or two after you do? The Eastern churches follow the *Julian* calendar, devised by Julius Caesar in 46 BC. Its calculations were inaccurate, and the dates began to creep up on the vernal equinox (when the sun crosses the equator northward) that determines the date of Easter. In 1582, Pope Gregory XIII dropped ten days from the current year to even things out and changed the leap-year rules to keep the errors from recurring. The Western church adopted this *Gregorian* calendar, but the Orthodox churches never accepted it, and its liturgical year runs thirteen days behind that of the West.

❦ THE SIGNERS OF THE DECLARATION OF ❦ INDEPENDENCE AND THEIR RELIGIOUS AFFILIATIONS

Name	State	Denomination
John Adams	Massachusetts	Congregational (Unitarian)
Samuel Adams	Massachusetts	Congregational
Josiah Bartlett	New Hampshire	Congregational
Carter Braxton	Virginia	Church of England
Charles Carroll of Carrollton	Maryland	Roman Catholic
Samuel Chase	Maryland	Church of England
Abraham Clark	New Jersey	Presbyterian
George Clymer	Pennsylvania	Quaker/Church of England
William Ellery	Rhode Island	Congregational
William Floyd	New York	Presbyterian
Benjamin Franklin	Pennsylvania	Deist* (buried Episcopal)**
Elbridge Gerry	Massachusetts	Church of England
Button Gwinnett	Georgia	Church of England
Lyman Hall	Georgia	Congregational
John Hancock	Massachusetts	Congregational
Benjamin Harrison	Virginia	Unknown
John Hart	New Jersey	Presbyterian
Joseph Hewes	North Carolina	Church of England
Thomas Heyward Jr.	South Carolina	Unknown
William Hooper	North Carolina	Church of England
Stephen Hopkins	Rhode Island	Unknown
Francis Hopkinson	New Jersey	Church of England
Samuel Huntington	Connecticut	Congregational
Thomas Jefferson	Virginia	Deist
Francis Lightfoot Lee	Virginia	Unknown
Richard Henry Lee	Virginia	Unknown
Francis Lewis	New York	Unknown
Philip Livingston	New York	Presbyterian
Thomas Lynch Jr.	South Carolina	Unknown
Thomas McKean	Delaware	Presbyterian
Arthur Middleton	South Carolina	Unknown
Lewis Morris	New York	Unknown
Robert Morris	Pennsylvania	Church of England
John Morton	Pennsylvania	Unknown
Thomas Nelson Jr.	Virginia	Unknown
William Paca	Maryland	Church of England
Robert Treat Paine	Massachusetts	Congregational
John Penn	North Carolina	Unknown

❧ THE SIGNERS OF THE DECLARATION OF ❧ INDEPENDENCE AND THEIR RELIGIOUS AFFILIATIONS—CONT.

Name	State	Denomination
George Read	Delaware	Church of England
Caesar Rodney	Delaware	Church of England
George Ross	Pennsylvania	Unknown
Benjamin Rush	Pennsylvania	Presbyterian
Edward Rutledge	South Carolina	Church of England
Roger Sherman	Connecticut	Congregational
James Smith	Pennsylvania	Presbyterian
Richard Stockton	New Jersey	Presbyterian
Thomas Stone	Maryland	Church of England
George Taylor	Pennsylvania	Presbyterian
Matthew Thornton	New Hampshire	Presbyterian
George Walton	Georgia	Church of England
William Whipple	New Hampshire	Congregational
William Williams	Connecticut	Congregational
James Wilson	Pennsylvania	Church of England/Deist
John Witherspoon	New Jersey	Presbyterian
Oliver Wolcott	Connecticut	Congregational
George Wythe	Virginia	Church of England

*Deism is a belief that God, having created the universe, does not interfere in its regular operation or in historical events, nor does he reveal truth except through the natural order. During the eighteenth century, some thinkers held this view while still maintaining a nominal membership in a Christian church.

**The Episcopal Church was organized after the Revolutionary War as the successor to the Church of England in the United States.

❧ THE FOUR EVANGELISTS (GOSPEL WRITERS) ❧

Matthew
(Winged Man)

Mark
(Winged Lion)

Luke
(Winged Ox)

John
(Eagle)

❧ MUSLIM BELIEFS ABOUT JESUS ❧

The Qur'an mentions Jesus (usually called *Isa* in Islam) several times, giving him honored titles. These are some of its teachings, implied or expressed, about him.

Jesus was a prophet, but only one of a succession of prophets culminating in Muhammad. Jesus cannot be the Son of God because Allah is One and can have no son.

Jesus is called the *Word* and the *Messiah*. Angels told Mary, "God gives thee good tidings of a Word from him whose name is Messiah, Jesus, son of Mary."

Jesus is God's messenger and his Spirit. "The Messiah Jesus Christ Son of Mary was only the messenger of God and his word that he committed unto Mary, and a Spirit from him."

Jesus was raised up to God. The Qur'an quotes him saying, "Peace be upon me, the day I was born, and the day I die, and the day I am raised up alive!"

But Jesus did not die on the cross; "only a likeness was shown" to his enemies. Muslims take this to mean that God made someone else appear to be Jesus and allowed him to be crucified, while Jesus was taken up to heaven without having died. A true prophet cannot fail.

Jesus denied the Trinity. He refused to claim, "Take me and my mother as gods, apart from God." Muhammad knew only a distorted form of Christianity and misunderstood the Trinity as God, Jesus, and Mary.

❧ TEN PLAGUES OF EGYPT ❧

1. Water of the Nile turned to blood (Exod. 7:20)
2. Frogs covering the land (Exod. 8:6)
3. Gnats covering the land and its creatures (Exod. 8:17)
4. Flies ruining the land (Exod. 8:24)
5. A plague destroying cattle and other animals (Exod. 9:6)
6. Boils or sores on people and animals (Exod. 9:10)
7. Hailstorm (Exod. 9:23)
8. Locusts destroying all plants (Exod. 10:13–15)
9. Darkness for three days (Exod. 10:22)
10. Death of the firstborn of people and cattle (Exod. 12:29)

❧ TWELVE APOSTLES OR SIXTEEN? ❧

Jesus had twelve disciples, but we know a larger number of people, including some women (Mark 15:40–41; Luke 23:55), were associated with him in his work. Because Jesus was calling Israel back to its true faith in God, there had to be *twelve* designated apostles as a symbol of the fullness of the twelve tribes. But the membership in this group may have been a bit fluid, since we have at least fifteen names plus Matthias, who was enrolled after the Resurrection:

1. Simon (Bar-Jonah, Matt. 16:17, also called Peter)
2. Andrew, brother of Simon
3. James, son of Zebedee
4. John, son of Zebedee
5. Philip
6. Bartholomew
7. Thomas (called the Twin, John 20:24)
8. Matthew
9. James, son of Alphaeus
10. Thaddaeus
11. Simon the Cananaean (or Zealot, Luke 6:15)
12. Judas Iscariot
13. Levi (Luke 5:27, usually equated with Matthew)
14. Nathanael of Cana
15. Judas, son of James (Luke 6:16; "not Iscariot," John 14:22)
16. Matthias (replacing Judas Iscariot, Acts 1:26)

❧ WHAT'S SO SPECIAL ABOUT THE TRIBE OF ❧ BENJAMIN'S LEFT-HANDED SLINGSHOTS?

Judges 20:15–16 states, "And the Benjaminites mustered out of their cities on that day twenty-six thousand men that drew the sword, besides the inhabitants of Gibeah, who mustered seven hundred picked men. Among all these were seven hundred picked men who were left-handed; every one could sling a stone at a hair, and not miss."

Why was it important to sling a shot with your left hand? This is one theory: To conquer a walled city, you had to break through its gate. As you faced the gate from outside, the ramp to it sloped up from the right along the wall. If you could creep up the ramp close to the wall, it was harder for the defenders to hit you with arrows or spears, but that kept your right arm too close to the wall to use a weapon. Now, if you were *left-handed*—you get the picture.

❧ WHY TWELVE TRIBES? ❧

The number twelve is significant in the Bible as a symbol for the fullness of Israel. The twenty-four (twelve plus twelve) elders of the Revelation to John probably represent the fullness of all believers, both of the old covenant and the new (symbolized in Jesus' twelve apostles). But why were there twelve Israelite tribes in the first place? Yes, Jacob their ancestor had twelve sons. But Simeon's land was included in that of Judah, so Joseph's tribe was split into territories for his sons Ephraim and Manasseh to make up twelve. The number was important.

Ancient Mediterranean peoples sometimes formed groups around a sanctuary (scholars call such a group an *amphictyony*). Israelites had a sanctuary, the tabernacle, which they moved about until they permanently located it in Jerusalem. Worship in the sanctuary required animals for sacrifice and other supplies, to be provided by the tribes belonging to the confederation. Since the year has *twelve* months (based on the lunar cycle), perhaps each tribe was responsible for the sanctuary for one month of the year. Psalm 81:3–4 might refer to this twelve-month system: "Blow the trumpet at the new moon, / at the full moon, on our feast day. / For it is a statute for Israel, / an ordinance of the God of Jacob."

❧ THE SERENITY PRAYER ❧

"God grant us the serenity to accept the things we cannot change, courage to change the things we can, and wisdom to know the difference."

This is the Serenity Prayer, popularized through the work of Alcoholics Anonymous. Where it came from is still a mystery. Alcoholics Anonymous picked it up from a 1942 obituary in a New York newspaper. Protestant theologian Reinhold Niebuhr (1892–1971) later revealed he had written it as the ending of a sermon. After his death a similar prayer was found in the writings of Theodor Wilhelm, a German university professor who published using the name of the eighteenth-century Pietist Friedrich Oetinger (1702–1782). A similar prayer came to light appearing to be derived from a fourteenth-century source called the General's Prayer.

❧ HEAVEN: FACT OR FICTION? ❧

A recent U.S. poll found

81 percent believed in heaven	8 percent didn't believe in heaven
10 percent weren't sure	1 percent had no opinion

❀ THE SEVEN . . . NO, THREE . . . ❀
OR IS IT TWO? . . . SACRAMENTS

Since the early Christian centuries, believers have thought of certain actions as *mysteries*, special signs of the gospel of Christ at work in the life of his church. The Greek word *musterion* was translated into the Latin *sacramentum*, with the implication of an action sacred in itself. A sacrament came to be defined as "an outward and visible sign of an inward and spiritual grace." Protestants began to think differently about these special acts, and in many churches they are limited to actions expressly instituted by Jesus.

Roman Catholic and Orthodox churches recognize the first seven acts on this list as sacraments (or mysteries). Many Anglicans recognize the third through seventh as "minor sacraments." Most Protestants recognize only the first two, and evangelical Protestants usually call them *ordinances* of Christ. Since Jesus also commended foot washing (John 13:14), some communities, such as the Brethren, regard this act as an ordinance.

1. Eucharist (Holy Communion, Lord's Supper)
2. Baptism
3. Confirmation (Chrismation)
4. Confession (Penance, Reconciliation)
5. Marriage
6. Holy Orders (Ordination)
7. Holy Unction (Anointing of the Sick)
8. Foot Washing (Humility)

❀ HOW DID THE MASS BECOME THE MASS? ❀

In the oldest Roman liturgies, once the Communion was over, a deacon announced, *"Ite missa est,"* or "Go, it's the dismissal." The response was, *"Deo gratias,"* "Thanks be to God." Because the words *Ite missa est* came at the end, they signified that the Holy Communion was complete. Hence the term *missa* came to stand for the entire rite of the Eucharist. In popular Latin it became *messa* and passed into Middle English in the form *mæsse,* or Mass.

❀ CHRISTIANS WHO WON'T VOTE ❀

Some Christian, or Christian-derived, groups in North America encourage their members not to vote. They view voting as taking responsibility for an ungodly society. These groups include the Amish, Hutterites, and Jehovah's Witnesses.

❧ THE WEST HAS ROME; THE EAST HAS . . . ❧

Catholics around the world look to the Holy Father in Rome for direction.
Orthodox Christians have five patriarchs with a similar symbolic role.

Patriarchate	Present Patriarch Installed	Comments
Constantinople	Bartholomew, 1991	Nominal head of all Orthodoxy but directly rules a tiny minority in a Muslim environment. Constantinople is now Istanbul.
Alexandria	Peter VI, 1997	Jurisdiction over Africa
Jerusalem	Irenaeus, 2002	Jurisdiction over Palestine
Antioch	Ignatius IV, 1979	Located in Damascus; jurisdiction over Syria and nearby regions
Moscow	Alexius II, 1991	—

The Orthodox churches are organized by nationality, with self-governing or *auto-cephalous* bodies nominally loyal to one of the five patriarchs and headed by a bishop called a *metropolitan*, *archbishop*, or other title. Originally Rome was one of the five patriarchates, but it developed into the Roman Catholic Church.

❧ THE TRADITIONAL WAY TO PRAY ❧ THROUGH THE DAY

The early Christians followed Jewish practice in setting specified hours through the day for prayer. Christian monks—who were lay, not clergy—developed this schedule, and Benedict (480–550) refined it. These hours of prayer are usually called the *Daily Office*, and each hour includes psalms, Scripture readings, regular prayers, and other material.

Matins .... Middle of the night, or before retiring

Lauds .... After Matins, or early morning

Prime (first) ..... Around 6:00 AM

Terce (third) .... Around 9:00 AM

Sext (sixth) ...... Around noon

None (ninth) .... Around 3:00 AM

Vespers .... Before dark

Compline .... Before retiring

❀ BRANCHES OF JUDAISM ❀

What does it mean to be Jewish? An ancient Jew, the apostle Paul, grappled with this issue in his letter to the Romans, and today's Jews still struggle with it. Judaism in North America is not monolithic; several definable movements exist within the Jewish community.

Branch	Description	Representative Institution
Orthodox	Holds to observance of the Torah (books of Moses), the kosher food laws, male headship, and other traditional practices	Rabbinical Council of America
Reformed	The "liberal" branch, seeks to adapt Judaism to the modern world; synagogues are called *temples*	Central Conference of American Rabbis
Conservative	Pursues a middle way between Orthodox and Reformed Judaism	United Synagogue of America
Hasidic	An extreme form of Jewish orthodoxy focusing on cabala, a medieval mystical and meditative tradition	Many small groups centered around a teacher called a *rebbe*
Reconstructionist	Views Judaism as a religious culture arising from a humanistic outlook, not given by God	Jewish Reconstructionist Federation
Messianic	Accepts Jesus as Messiah but practices a form of Judaism; other Jews do not consider them Jewish	Many missionary organizations such as Jews for Jesus, plus local congregations

❀ THE MOST TRAVELED PREACHER EVER ❀ ... AND THE RUNNER-UP

John Wesley, founder of the Methodist movement, rode 250,000 miles in England on horseback and preached 42,000 sermons. Francis Asbury, whom Wesley appointed to organize Methodism in the United States, outrode him. He covered 300,000 miles, but in sparsely settled America he preached only 16,000 sermons.

❋ GREAT PREACHERS OF CHRISTIAN HISTORY ❋

Great preachers have always motivated the Christian community, and some of them have been remembered throughout history.

Preacher	Dates	Locations	Denomination
Ambrose of Milan	330–397	North Italy	Ancient church
John Chrysostom	344–407	Antioch and Constantinople	Ancient church
Peter the Hermit	1050–1115	Northeastern France	Catholic
Bernard of Clairvaux	1090–1153	Eastern France	Catholic
Dominic de Guzman	1170–1221	Spain, France	Catholic
Girolamo Savonarola	1452–1498	Florence	Catholic
John Wesley	1703–1791	England	Anglican (Methodist)
George Whitefield	1714–1770	England, American colonies	Anglican (Calvinistic Methodist)
Lyman Beecher	1775–1863	Litchfield, CT, and Cincinnati	Congregational
Theodore Parker	1810–1860	Boston	Unitarian
Charles Haddon Spurgeon	1834–1892	London	Baptist
Phillips Brooks	1835–1893	Boston	Episcopal
Harry Emerson Fosdick	1878–1969	New York City	Baptist, non-denominational
Helmut Thielicke	1908–1986	Germany	Evangelical church
Fulton J. Sheen	1895–1979	New York City	Catholic
Norman Vincent Peale	1898–1993	New York City	Reformed
D. Martyn Lloyd-Jones	1899–1981	London	Congregational
Billy Graham	1918–	—	Baptist

❋ THE FISH SYMBOL ❋

The Greek word for "fish," *ichthys*, has five letters (*ch* and *th* are each one letter in Greek). The five letters are the first letters of the expression "Jesus Christ, Son of God, Savior" in Greek.

Fish—Jesus Christ

ΙΧΘΥϹ

❀ CHURCHES THAT LOOK ORTHODOX ❀
BUT ARE CATHOLIC

The church has an onion-shaped dome, the liturgy is in some old language other than Latin, the "ambience" is that of an Orthodox church—yet the church is actually Catholic, in communion with the pope. Churches like this are called *Eastern Rite Catholic* or *Uniate* churches. They use one of the several ancient Eastern liturgies that their Orthodox counterparts also use, especially the Byzantine Liturgy of St. John Chrysostom. Often their priests are married, which Roman priests aren't.

Rite	Rite Type	Main Countries of Origin	Typical Language
Armenian	Armenian	Armenia, Turkey	Classical Armenian
Chaldean	Chaldean	Iraq	Syriac, Arabic
Coptic	Alexandrian	Egypt	Coptic, Arabic
Ge'ez	Alexandrian	Ethiopia	Ge'ez
Greek	Byzantine	Greece, Turkey	Greek
Malankar	Antiochene	India	Syriac, Malayalam
Maronite	Antiochene	Lebanon	Syriac, Arabic
Melkite	Byzantine	Syria, Lebanon	Arabic
Russian	Byzantine	Russia	Old Slavonic
Ruthenian (Carpatho-Russian)	Byzantine	Slovakia, Hungary	Old Slavonic
Ukrainian	Byzantine	Ukraine	Old Slavonic, Ukrainian
Syrian	Antiochene	Lebanon, Iraq	Syriac, Arabic
Syro-Malabar	Chaldean	India	Syriac, Malayalam

❀ THE FIVE FUNDAMENTALS OF FUNDAMENTALISM ❀

Fundamentalism arose from a statement conservative Christians issued at the Niagara Bible Conference of 1895. These leaders were concerned about trends in the major denominations of North America that they felt were departures from biblical Christianity. The five "fundamentals of the faith" that gave fundamentalism its name are these:

1. The inerrancy of Scripture
2. The deity and the virgin birth of Jesus Christ
3. The substitutionary atonement (i.e., Christ died for our sins)
4. The bodily resurrection of Jesus
5. The personal return of Christ

❆ DIFFERENT VERSIONS OF THE LORD'S PRAYER ❆

Many churches in North America regularly use the Lord's Prayer in worship, though most evangelical and Pentecostal churches do not. Catholics call it the "Our Father," as do Anglicans and others on occasion. When attending a church other than your own, it's a good idea to be alert to its favorite version of the prayer Jesus taught his disciples:

> Our Father who art in heaven,
> Hallowed be thy name,
> Thy kingdom come,
> Thy will be done,
>   On earth as it is in heaven.
> Give us this day our daily bread;
> And forgive us our debts,
>   As we also have forgiven our debtors;
> And lead us not into temptation,
>   But deliver us from evil. (Matthew 6:9–13)

Catholic, Lutheran, Anglican/Episcopal, United Methodist, and some other denominations say, "Forgive us our trespasses as we forgive those who trespass against us." Baptist, Presbyterian, Christian, and evangelical churches are more likely to say, "Forgive us our debts, as we forgive our debtors."

Catholic worshipers end the prayer with "but deliver us from evil." (It is part of the Eucharistic Prayer before Communion.) Protestants continue with the doxology, "For thine is the kingdom and the power and the glory . . ."

Anglicans, Episcopalians, and Lutherans say, ". . . forever and ever. Amen." Everyone else usually says, ". . . forever. Amen."

A few churches use a version in more contemporary wording, though most stick with the "thy, thine" form.

If the prayer is sung, some of the wording may change. It's easier to sing, "Forgive us our sins, as we forgive those who sin against us."

❆ THE CITIES OF THE DECAPOLIS ❆

The Decapolis was a federation of ten Greek-speaking cities in the region east of the Sea of Galilee and the Jordan River. Jesus preached in the Decapolis (Mark 5:20; 7:31). The cities were

Abila • Canatha • Dion • Gadara • Gerasa • Hippos
Pella • Philadelphia • Raphana • Scythopolis

❧ CHURCHES THAT ARE NOT CATHOLIC, ❧ ORTHODOX, OR PROTESTANT

"Gallia est omnis divisa in partes tres," wrote Julius Caesar—"All Gaul is divided in three parts." Usually we think of Christianity the same way: you are either Protestant, Catholic, or Orthodox. Not so. Here are several ancient and still existing churches that were never part of the "big three."

Church	Origin	Head and Where Located	Comments
Abyssinian	Ethiopia	Abuna (Patriarch), Addis Ababa	The independent Coptic church of Ethiopia; follows many Jewish practices
Armenian	Armenia	Catholicos, Etchmiadzin	Armenia was the first nation to officially adopt Christianity, in 301.
Coptic	Egypt	Pope, Cairo	The ancient Christian church of Egypt; headed by its own pope
Jacobite	Syria, Iraq, India	Patriarch of Antioch, Damascus	Also called *Oriental Orthodox*
Nestorian	Iraq, Iran, India	Catholicos Patriarch, Chicago	Now a remnant; was the dominant Christian church of central Asia before Muslim expansion; sometimes called *Assyrian Church* or *Church of the East*

❧ THE ORIGIN OF THE TERM *DEVIL'S ADVOCATE* ❧

In the Roman Catholic Church, when a person is proposed for sainthood, the first big step is to have him or her declared "blessed," or *beatified*. Before this can happen, church officials conduct an investigation to see if any significant reasons exist for why that person should not be *canonized* as a saint. The official whose job it is to raise all possible objections is called the "promoter of the faith," but he is popularly styled the "devil's advocate." Catholic canon law requires that someone recognized as a saint should have led a holy life and that miracles should be associated with him or her, either while living or after death. If the "devil's advocate" isn't convincing enough in his objections, then the way is cleared for eventual canonization.

❦ POPES WITH THE SHORTEST REIGNS ❦

Pope	Year	Held Office
Urban VII	1590	13 days
Boniface VI	896	16 days
Celestine IV	1241	17 days
Sissinnius	708	21 days
Theodore II	897	21 days
Marcellus II	1555	22 days
Damasus II	1048	24 days
Pius III	1503	27 days
Leo XI	1605	27 days
Benedict V	964	33 days
John Paul I*	1978	34 days

*Karol Józef Wojtyla (John Paul II) took the name of his briefly reigning predecessor upon being elected pope.

❦ THE FIRST TWELVE TRANSLATIONS OF THE BIBLE ❦

1. Samaritan Pentateuch—Third or fourth century BC; not a translation, but a version of the Hebrew books of Moses in old Hebrew script

2. Septuagint (Greek)—Third to second centuries BC; there were multiple Greek versions of Old Testament books of which the Septuagint was most influential

3. Peshitta (Syriac)—Second-century translation of the Hebrew Scriptures with New Testament added later; still the authorized version of Syriac-speaking churches

4. Old Latin—Various translations made in the second to third centuries, surviving chiefly in quotations by the church fathers

5. Old Syriac (i.e., Aramaic)—Around 200; only Gospels survive

6. Sahidic (Coptic)—Around 200

7. Armenian—Third- to fourth-century translation of the New Testament, from Old Syriac

8. Gothic—Fourth century; only portions survive

9. Latin Vulgate—Completed 404 by Jerome; the authorized Roman Catholic version

10. Ethiopic (Ge'ez)—Fourth to fifth centuries

11. Philoxenian (Syriac)—508; only a few books survive

12. Georgian—Sixth century, translated from Armenian

❦ CHRISTIAN BESTSELLERS ❦

This list doesn't include the Bible, the all-time "bestseller." It is said that Bunyan's *Pilgrim's Progress* is second only to the Bible in the number of copies distributed, and that Sheldon's *In His Steps* has sold 28,500,000 copies.

Life of St. Antony, ascribed to Athansius, 360
The Imitation of Christ, Thomas à Kempis, 1425
Book of Martyrs (Acts and Monuments), John Foxe, 1563, later supplemented
Pilgrim's Progress, John Bunyan, 1678
The Christian's Secret of a Happy Life, Hannah Whitall Smith, 1875
Ben-Hur, Lew Wallace, 1880
In His Steps, Charles Monroe Sheldon, 1896
Quo Vadis? Henryk K. Sienkiewicz, 1896
The Robe, Lloyd Douglas, 1942
God's Smuggler, Brother Andrew (Andy van der Bijl), 1967
The Late Great Planet Earth, Hal Lindsey, 1970
The Purpose-Driven Life, Rick Warren, 2002
The Left Behind series, Tim LaHaye and Jerry B. Jenkins, 1995–2004

❦ THE CHALCEDONIAN CREED ❦

The Chalcedonian Creed, from the Council of Chalcedon (451), is not used in worship.

We, then, following the holy Fathers, all with one consent, teach men to confess one and the same Son, our Lord Jesus Christ, the same perfect in Godhead and also perfect in manhood; truly God and truly man, of a reasonable soul and body; consubstantial with the Father according to the Godhead, and consubstantial with us according to the Manhood; in all things like unto us, without sin; begotten before all ages of the Father according to the Godhead, and in these latter days, for us and for our salvation, born of the Virgin Mary, the Mother of God, according to the Manhood; one and the same Christ, Son, Lord, only begotten, to be acknowledged in two natures, inconfusedly, unchangeably, indivisibly, inseparably; the distinction of natures being by no means taken away by the union, but rather the property of each nature being preserved, and concurring in one Person and one Subsistence, not parted or divided into two persons, but one and the same Son, and only begotten, God the Word, the Lord Jesus Christ; as the prophets from the beginning [have declared] concerning Him, and the Lord Jesus Christ Himself has taught us, and the Creed of the holy Fathers has handed down to us. (Traditional English version)

❧ ONWARD CHRISTIAN SOLDIERS: ❧
THE CRUSADES OF CHRISTENDOM

Muslim Arabs captured Jerusalem in 637, but Christian pilgrimages to the Holy Land continued. In 1071, however, the more hostile Seljuk Turks took Jerusalem and went on to conquer most of Asia Minor, weakening the eastern Roman Empire. After an appeal from the emperor Alexius I Comnenus, Pope Urban II (ruled 1088–1099) urged an expedition to recover the Holy Land. These are the crusades that followed, as commonly reckoned.

First Crusade (1096–1099) . . . . Captured Antioch, established the Latin Kingdom of Jerusalem

Second Crusade (1147–1149) . . . . . No result; most crusaders never reached the Holy Land

Third Crusade (1188–1192) . . . . . Syrian ruler Saladin had recaptured Jerusalem in 1187; Richard I of England made a truce with him, allowing crusaders to visit Jerusalem

Fourth Crusade (1202–1204) . . . . . Never reached the Holy Land but placed a Latin ruler on the throne of the Eastern Empire in Constantinople

Children's Crusade (1212) . . . . Few children even reached the ports of France and Italy; perhaps the origin of the legend of the "Pied Piper."

Fifth Crusade (1217–1221) . . . . Took place mostly in Egypt, recovered the Holy Cross (supposed true cross)

Sixth Crusade (1228-1229) . . . . Frederick II (Holy Roman Emperor) governed Jerusalem for fifteen years, till its final recapture by the Turks in 1244.

Seventh Crusade (1248–1254) . . . . Louis IX of France strengthened some Christian enclaves in Syria but could not retake Jerusalem.

Eighth Crusade (1270) . . . . Louis IX attacked Tunis but died there; soon the remaining Christian enclaves in Syria were lost to Islam.

The Holy Land finally passed again into Western hands during World War I, when British General Edmund Allenby captured it from the Ottoman Turks in 1917–1918.

❧ BIBLICAL WOMEN NAMED MARY ❧

In the Bible, the name *Mary* is *Miriam* in the Old Testament, *Mariam, Marias,* or *Maria* in the New Testament. These are the eight or nine women of the Bible bearing that name:

Miriam	Sister of Moses and Aaron
Miriam	Daughter of Mered and Bithiah, the daughter of Pharaoh (1 Chron. 4:17)
Mary	Mother of Jesus
Mary Magdalene	Miriam of Magdala
The "other" Mary	Mother of James and Joses (Matt. 27:61)
Mary	Wife of Clopas (John 19:25, may be same as above)
Mary	Sister of Martha and Lazarus
Mary	Mother of John Mark (Acts 12:12)
Mary	Greeted by Paul in Romans 16:6

❧ THE SEVEN LAST WORDS OF CHRIST ❧

The traditional Seven Last Words of Christ on the cross are these, from the Revised Standard Version:

1. "Father, forgive them; for they know not what they do" (Luke 23:34).
2. "Woman, behold, your son!" (John 19:26).
3. "Truly, I say to you, today you will be with me in Paradise" (Luke 23:43).
4. "I thirst" (John 19:28).
5. "My God, my God, why hast thou forsaken me?" (Matt. 27:46; Mark 15:34).
6. "Father, into thy hands I commit my spirit!" (Luke 23:46).
7. "It is finished" (John 19:30).

These were not Jesus' *last* words, of course. His last words before his ascension into heaven were: "It is not for you to know times or seasons which the Father has fixed by his own authority. But you shall receive power when the Holy Spirit has come upon you; and you shall be my witnesses in Jerusalem and in all Judea and Samaria and to the end of the earth" (Acts 1:7–8).

His last recorded words to the apostle Paul were: "Take courage, for as you have testified about me at Jerusalem, so you must bear witness also at Rome" (Acts 23:11).

His last recorded words to the apostle John were: "Surely I am coming soon" (Rev. 22:20).

❧ THE UNFORTUNATE WIVES OF HENRY VIII ❧

England's King Henry VIII (ruled 1509–1547) broke with the Church of Rome in part over the issue of divorce. His first wife, Catherine of Aragon, bore him only one child who survived, a daughter. Catherine had been the widow of Henry's older brother Arthur, and Henry became convinced from a passage in Leviticus that their marriage was invalid. When the pope refused to grant an annulment, Henry made himself the head of the church in England and had Archbishop Thomas Cranmer annul the marriage. (In 1556, Cranmer was martyred by Catherine's daughter Mary, known as "Bloody Mary," in her effort to return England to the Catholic fold.)

Catherine of Aragon	Marriage annulled 1533	Mother of Mary I (ruled 1553–1558)
Anne Boleyn	Executed 1536	Mother of Elizabeth I (ruled 1558–1603)
Jane Seymour	Died 1537	Mother of Edward VI (ruled 1547–1553)
Anne of Cleves	Marriage annulled 1540	
Catherine Howard	Executed 1542	
Catherine Parr	Survived	

❧ THE SEVEN CHURCH COUNCILS ❧

Both the Catholic and Orthodox churches recognize seven ancient councils of the church, called the *Ecumenical Councils* (from the Greek *oikumene*, "inhabited world"). Some of the non-Orthodox Eastern churches recognize only the first three. The Anglican and Reformed traditions honor the councils but apply the test of Scripture to their deliberations. These are the Ecumenical Councils and the issues they dealt with. For a description of the issues, see the entries on *Heretics and Their Heresies* and *Obscure Chrisian -Isms*.

1. Nicaea, 325 . . . . Arianism
2. Constantinople I, 381 . . . . Apollinarianism
3. Ephesus, 431 . . . . Nestorianism
4. Chalcedon, 451 . . . . Eutychianism
5. Constantinople II, 553 . . . . Three Chapters Controversy (views of writers sympathetic to Nestorius)
6. Constantinople III, 680–681 . . . . . Monothelitism
7. Nicaea II, 787 . . . . Iconoclasm

❦ POPULAR BIBLICAL NAMES FOR CHILDREN ❦

There are twelve Bible names among the current top twenty for boys, whereas the top twenty for girls include only six. Some girls' names are feminine versions of boys' names (Danielle, Gabrielle), while a number of them represent biblical virtues or qualities (Grace; Faith; Zoe, the New Testament Greek word for *life*; Sophia, the word for *wisdom*). Madeline is from Mary Magdalene, and Jordan is the river. The Godhead does better on the feminine side; Trinity ranks fifty-seventh among girls, whereas Jesus is sixty-fifth among boys. If, however, you include ninth-ranked Christopher (which means "Christ-bearer") and twenty-third-ranked Christian, the boys do much better. Some names exist in multiple versions, partly due to ethnic variations.

Boys		*Girls*	
Jacob or James	Alexander	Sarah or Sara	Julia
Joseph or José	Zachary	Hannah	Jordan
Michael	Jonathan	Abigail	Faith
John or Juan	Samuel	Elizabeth	Trinity
Joshua	Christian	Grace	Zoe
Matthew	Benjamin	Maria or Mary	Madeline
Andrew	Nathan	Sophia	Rebecca
Ethan	Gabriel	Anna	Leah
Daniel	Noah	Chloe	Danielle
David	Caleb	Rachel	Gabrielle, Gabriella, or Gabriela

❦ CHURCH CANDLES ❦

The use of candles in Christian worship began with the custom of carrying candles in procession before the bishop of Rome (pope), then placing them around the altar. Beginning around the year 1200, worshipers actually placed candles on the altar, and the custom spread throughout the church. In Catholic and other churches, worshipers place smaller votive candles before statues of saints or on a special rack. This use of candles may go back to Israelite practice, in which a lamp stand (using oil lamps, not candles) was placed in the sanctuary.

Today candles have come to symbolize Christ, "the Light of the World," Christ's offering of himself (as the candle burns down), or a prayer request. Probably their original purpose was none of these. Ancient churches were built of stone, with thick walls and few windows until the Gothic churches of the Middle Ages. It was quite dark inside the church, even in daytime. Candles were needed for their light, if nothing else.

❊ CHRISTIAN ACRONYMS AND ABBREVIATIONS ❊

AD . . . . Anno Domini, The Year of Our Lord

CE . . . . Of the Common Era

B.V.M. . . . . Blessed Virgin Mary

COGIC . . . . Church of God in Christ

IFCA . . . . Independent Fundamental Churches of America

ECFA . . . . Evangelical Council on Fiscal Accountability

ECUSA . . . . Episcopal Church (USA)

EFCA . . . . Evangelical Free Church of America

KJV . . . . King James Version

NAE . . . . National Association of Evangelicals

NIV . . . . New International Version

NT . . . . New Testament

O.P. . . . . Order of Preachers (Dominicans)

O.S.B. . . . . Order of St. Benedict (Benedictines)

OT . . . . Old Testament

PCUSA . . . . Presbyterian Church (USA)

RV . . . . Revised Version (English, 1881)

RSV . . . . Revised Standard Version

SBC . . . . Southern Baptist Convention

S.J. . . . . Society of Jesus (Jesuits)

UCC . . . . United Church of Christ

❊ EARMARKS OF A "CHRISTIAN" CULT ❊

What makes a religious movement a cult? Analysts offer several criteria for labeling a movement a cult:

- Teachings that modify, or go beyond, clear statements of Scripture.

- Sacred or special writings or traditions that reinterpret or supersede the Bible.

- Manipulation of members or potential members (condemnation for anyone who leaves the movement or questions its teaching).

- A controlling authority structure, often with one idolized leader.

- An attitude of exclusiveness: "We are the only true church with the only truth."

❧ OF CATHEDRALS AND BASILICAS ❧

In North America a large, imposing church is sometimes called a *cathedral*—such as the Washington National Cathedral or Robert Schuller's Crystal Cathedral in Garden Grove, California. The name *cathedral*, however, comes from the Latin word *cathedra*, meaning "throne." A church is correctly called a cathedral only if a bishop is "seated" there, as in the Catholic, Orthodox, or Anglican traditions. Even a small building can be a cathedral if it is the bishop's church.

Basilica, Dyersville, Iowa

The term *basilica* is derived from the Greek word for "king." In the Roman world, basilicas were large, oblong halls in major cities where the emperor held court when visiting. The church took over the basilica as its favored building style. Today, however, the Roman Catholic Church designates a church or cathedral as a basilica if it has a unique ceremonial role or special historical or architectural merit. Examples are the Basilica of St. Thérèse in Lisieux, France, devoted to the veneration of this saint, or the Basilica of the Agony in the Garden of Gethsemane at Jerusalem. There are at least thirty-seven basilicas in the United States, such as the Basilica of the National Shrine of the Assumption of the Blessed Virgin Mary in Baltimore, and the Basilica of Saint Francis Xavier in the small town of Dyersville, Iowa. Canada has at least nine, including the Basilica-Cathedral of Notre Dame in the old city of Quebec.

❧ THE APOSTLES' CREED ❧

The Apostles' Creed, or "Roman Symbol," is a fourth-century baptismal creed.

> *I believe in God the Father Almighty, Maker of heaven and earth; and in Jesus Christ his only Son our Lord, who was conceived by the Holy Ghost, born of the Virgin Mary, suffered under Pontius Pilate, was crucified, dead, and buried. He descended into hell; the third day he rose again from the dead. He ascended into heaven, and sitteth on the right hand of God the Father Almighty; from thence he shall come to judge the quick and the dead.*
>
> *I believe in the Holy Ghost, the holy catholic Church, the communion of saints, the forgiveness of sins, the resurrection of the body and the life everlasting. Amen.*
> (Book of Common Prayer, *1928*)

❋ RIVERS OF THE BIBLE ❋

The Bible often mentions rivers and streams, vital in a region of sporadic rainfall. These are some of the most important.

Tigris . . . . One of the four rivers of Eden, along with the following

Euphrates . . . . The "great river" (Gen. 15:18) or simply "the River" (Gen. 31:21 NIV), considered the boundary between Mesopotamia* and areas to the west "Beyond the River" (Ezra 6:8)

River of Egypt . . . . . Probably a *wadi* or torrential stream that divided Egypt from the land of Israel (Gen. 15:18)

Jabbok . . . . Where Jacob wrestled and his name was changed to Israel (Gen. 32)

Nile . . . . Where Pharaoh's daughter found the baby Moses (Exod. 2); he turned its waters into blood (Exod. 7)

Jordan . . . . Divides the Promised Land into areas known historically as "Trans-Jordan" and "Cis-Jordan" (West Bank). Joshua led the Israelites across it, and Jesus was baptized in it.

Abana and Pharpar . . The rivers of Damascus that Naaman thought were more impressive than the Jordan (2 Kings 5)

Kishon . . . . The brook where Elijah slew the prophets of Baal (1 Kings 18)

Chebar . . . . In Mesopotamia, where Ezekiel had his visions

River in the . . . . The "river whose streams make glad the city of God" (Ps. 46:4 NIV). The Kidron in Jerusalem
"city of God"   is a small brook, so this river is a visionary one, perhaps the same as the following.

River of Life . . . . The visionary river flowing from the sanctuary (Ezek. 47); the river in the new Jerusalem (Rev. 22). Jesus spoke of the "rivers of living water" flowing from the life of the believer (John 7:38).

Rivers in the desert . . Isaiah 43, perhaps the same as above

Mesopotamia means "between the rivers," a Greek name for the area known as Babylon or Chaldea (modern Iraq).

❦ YOUR RELIGIOUS NEIGHBORS ❦

Religious groups are not evenly distributed across the United States. The denominational preferences of your neighbors are likely to change depending on what part of the country you live in.

- If you live in New England, New York, New Jersey, most of Pennsylvania, or anywhere near the Great Lakes, your neighbors will probably be Catholic.

- If you live in Delaware, Maryland, central Pennsylvania, the northern part of West Virginia, southern Ohio, Indiana, central Illinois, southern Iowa, Nebraska, or Kansas, there is a good chance your neighbors are Methodists.

- If you live in Virginia, southern West Virginia, Kentucky, southern Illinois, Missouri, the Carolinas, Georgia, Tennessee, Arkansas, Oklahoma, Georgia, Alabama, Mississippi, northern Louisiana, most of Texas, or northern or central Florida, you will definitely have Baptist neighbors.

- If you live in south Florida, southern Louisiana, or near the Rio Grande Valley in Texas, your neighbors could well be Catholic.

- If you live in western Wisconsin, Minnesota, northern Iowa, the Dakotas, or eastern Montana, you will probably have Lutheran neighbors.

- If you live in western Montana, Wyoming, Colorado, New Mexico, Arizona, California, western Nevada, or Alaska, it is likely that your neighbors are Catholic.

- If you live in Utah, Idaho, or eastern Nevada, you will have Mormon neighbors.

- If you live in Washington State, Oregon, or Hawaii, your neighbors may not attend church at all.

❦ ORIGINS OF CHRISTMAS ❦

The New Testament contains no command to celebrate the birth of Jesus, and Scripture doesn't indicate the time of year when he was born. The traditional December 25 date came from a Roman winter festival, the *Natalis Solis Invicti*, a festival of the sun after the winter solstice when the days in the Northern Hemisphere begin to lengthen. Despite objections from early Christian theologians concerned about confusing Christ with the sun god, Christians had begun to celebrate the birth of Jesus on this day by the fourth century. Perhaps they felt this would keep weaker believers from falling back into the popular Roman custom.

❧ JOHN WESLEY'S "GENERAL RULES" ❧

For a preacher of God's free grace who irked his Calvinist critics, John Wesley was no slacker about living a methodical Christian life, and he expected the same commitment from his Methodist followers. In 1739 he formulated the General Rules of the "United Society," at the request of several who asked for help in "working out their own salvation" (see Phil. 2:12).

There is only one condition required of those who desire admission into these societies, a "desire to flee from the wrath to come, and to be saved from their sins." But wherever this is really fixed in the soul, it will be shown by its fruits. It is therefore expected of all who continue therein, that they shall continue to evidence their desire of salvation.

First, by doing no harm, by avoiding evil of every kind, especially that which is most generally practiced. . . .

Secondly, by doing good, by being in every kind merciful after their power as they have opportunity, doing good of every possible sort, and, as far as possible, to all men:

To their bodies, of the ability which God giveth; by giving food to the hungry; by clothing the naked, by visiting or helping them that are sick or in prison.

To their souls, by instructing, reproving, or exhorting all that we have any intercourse with; trampling under foot that enthusiastic doctrine that "We are not to do good unless our hearts be free to do it."

. . . By all possible diligence and frugality, that the gospel be not blamed. By running with patience the race set before them, denying themselves and taking up their cross daily; submitting to bear the reproach of Christ; to bear the filth and offscouring of the world; and looking that men should say all manner of evil of them for the Lord's sake.

Thirdly, by attending upon all these ordinances of God; which are,

The Public Worship of God;

The Ministry of the Word, either read or expounded;

The Supper of the Lord;

Family and private prayer;

Searching the Scriptures;

Fasting, or abstinence.

These are the General Rules of our Societies; all of which we are taught of God to observe, even in His written Word, which is the only rule, and the sufficient rule, both of our faith and practice. And all these we know his Spirit writes on truly awakened hearts. If there be any among us who observe them not, who habitually break any of them, let it be known unto them who watch over that soul, as they who must give an account. We all admonish him of the error of his ways: we will bear with him for a season; but then if he repent not, he hath no more place among us; we have delivered our own souls.

❊ SOME CHRISTIAN "OLOGIES" ❊

The suffix -ology comes from the Greek word logos ("word"), meaning the expression, science, or body of knowledge of a subject. These are some "ologies" and their subjects.

Angelology .... Angels

Bibliology .... The Bible

Christology .... The nature of Jesus Christ

Cosmology .... The universe

Ecclesiology .... The church

Epistemology .... How people know

Eschatology .... The "last things" or end times

Hagiology .... The saints

Hamartiology ...... The nature and extent of sin

Mariology .... The Virgin Mary

Martyrology .... Martyrs (a catalog or history)

Pneumatology ...... The Holy Spirit

Soteriology .... Salvation, or how Christ saves

Theology .... God

❊ CHRISTIAN FEASTS THAT CHANGE ❊ DAYS FROM YEAR TO YEAR

Christmas is always December 25 (in the Western church); why does the date of Easter change every year? Christians in the early centuries disagreed about the day for celebrating Christ's resurrection. Some wanted to observe it on the fourteenth of the Jewish month of Nisan, the day of Passover, while others argued for a schedule independent of the Jewish calendar. The bitter controversy quieted down after 325, when the Council of Nicaea determined that Easter should be celebrated on the first Sunday after the first full moon following the vernal equinox. The moon circles the earth in a twenty-eight-day cycle, so the date changes each year.

Some days of the church year depend on the date of Christmas. The Advent season begins the fourth Sunday before, while Epiphany Day is the twelfth day after Christmas. Other days, however, depend on the date of Easter. Ash Wednesday comes forty days before, not counting Sundays, and Pentecost is the fiftieth day (as its name means in Greek) afterward. This means that the Epiphany season expands or contracts with the changing dates of Ash Wednesday, and the Pentecost season varies in length at the other end of the "sliding" part of the liturgical year.

❀ CHRISTMAS TRADITIONS AROUND THE WORLD ❀

Aleuts (Alaska, U.S.) .... Celebrators eat *piruk* (fish pie) or smoked salmon; caroling children carry a colored star on a long pole.

Austria .... "St. Nicholas" gives sweets, toys, and nuts to children with a list of good deeds. Baked carp is the traditional Christmas dinner.

Bangladesh .... Worshipers light the way to church using arches made from banana trees, with oil lamps.

China .... Santa Claus is called "Christmas Old Man" (Dun Che Lao Ren).

Egypt .... Christians fast during Advent; on Christmas Eve (January 6) they attend church wearing new clothes, and on Christmas Day they visit friends and share *kaik*, a type of shortbread.

England .... Christmas dessert is a rich, fruity pudding with brandy sauce.

Ethiopia .... Christmas Eve worshipers circle the church three times with lighted candles; Christmas food includes *injera*, a sourdough bread.

France .... Children leave their shoes by the fireplace to be filled with gifts by Père Noël; players or puppeteers reenact the story of Christ's birth in church squares.

Germany .... Children leave letters on their window sills for Christkind, a winged figure in white robes bringing gifts; families bake gingerbread houses; in some homes, the Christmas tree and gifts are kept in a locked room, opened only on Christmas Day.

Greenland .... Celebrators eat *mattak*, whale skin containing a strip of blubber.

Iraq .... Families light a fire of dried thorns in their courtyard on Christmas Eve; if it burns to ashes, they will have a good year. Another bonfire is lit in church on Christmas Day, and there is a procession with an image of the child Jesus.

Ireland .... On the day after Christmas, St. Stephen's Day, there are football matches and other events; boys go from door to door with a fake wren on a stick, singing and playing instruments and asking for money "for the starving wren," actually for themselves.

❀ CHRISTMAS TRADITIONS AROUND THE WORLD—CONT. ❀

Labrador (Canada) . . . . Children are given turnips with a lighted candle.

Mexico . . . . La Posada is a procession reenacting Joseph and Mary's search for shelter before the birth of Jesus; celebrators go from house to house carrying their images. (Many Hispanic countries have the same custom.)

Netherlands . . . . Sinterklaas Eve, when St. Nicholas distributes gifts, is December 5.

Portugal . . . . Hoping to receive gifts and treats on January 6, children place their shoes, filled with carrots and straw, on window sills to lure the horses of the Magi.

Russia . . . . Babushka, or "Grandmother," is a legendary figure who distributes presents to children; she failed to go with the Magi but changed her mind and is still trying to find Jesus.

Sweden . . . . Christmas trees are set up only a day or two before Christmas; the Christmas goat (*julbok*) distributes the gifts; Christmas dinner includes *lutfisk* (boiled codfish).

❀ THE CHRISTIAN FLAG ❀

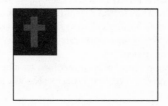

The Christian flag is one of the world's oldest unchanged flags. Charles C. Overton, a Sunday school superintendent on Staten Island, New York, designed it in 1897. When a guest speaker failed to appear, Overton noticed an American flag in the room and gave an impromptu talk on the meaning of flags. It suddenly occurred to him that there should be a Christian flag, and he designed the one still in use. The flag is white (for purity and peace), with a blue field (faithfulness, truth, and sincerity) and a red cross (the sacrifice of Christ). These colors are the same as the American flag but were also used in the Israelite tabernacle.

❊ A CHURCH BULLETIN FROM AD 150 ❊

What was early Christian worship like? The New Testament doesn't go into detail about it, but two sources from the following century begin to connect the dots. They are the anonymous *Didache* (dee-duh-KAY), or *Teaching of the Twelve Apostles,* and the *First Apology* of Justin Martyr. Justin was a lawyer who converted to Christianity and wrote a defense of the faith (traditionally called an *apology*) addressed to the Roman emperor. For his trouble he was put to death sometime around 165. Hence he's called Justin *Martyr*—that was not his last name.

Here's what the bulletin or "worship folder" might look like, combining what we know from our two sources.

First Church, Illyricum
Lord's Day XXII, Annum XII Caesar Antoninus Pius

Presider: Presbyter M. Diotrephes Demetrios
Deacons: F. Urbanus Cimber, Stephanos Philippos
Prophetess: Priscilla Lydia

Welcome to First Church. We're glad you came to worship with us on this Lord's Day. Please remember that only Christians baptized in the name of the Lord are invited to share in the Lord's Table. If you haven't received the "washing" for rebirth, please leave after the teaching time. We hope you'll understand and soon decide to become a Christian and take our membership training course.

Please remain standing for the entire service—men to the right, women to the left.

Our guest prophet today is Flavius Eumenes of Amphipolis. Please be generous in providing for his needs as he moves on toward Brundisium this week.

We thank the family of G. Archippus Pudens for opening their spacious home to our gathering this Lord's Day. We urge you to take care not to allow young people to sit on the window ledges—remember Eutychus!

The Thanksgiving Meal will be taken to members who are absent today due to illness or work; please remind the deacons of friends or family members who need to be visited.

The Writings
Read by Presbyter Demetrios
From the book of the prophet Isaiah
From the memoirs of the apostle Paul
From the memoirs of the apostle Matthew

Teaching from the Writings
Presbyter Demetrios

Hymn "My Soul Magnifies the Lord"
Led by the Prophets

❋ A CHURCH BULLETIN FROM AD 150—CONT. ❋

Prayers

Led by Deacon Philippos
You may join in offering prayers for your needs and those of others, especially for those baptized this week.

Kiss of Peace

Greet one another with a holy kiss. Please confine your greeting to your own (men's or women's) side of the room.

The Gifts

The deacons will present the bread, wine, and water.

Thanksgiving before the Meal

Presbyter Demetrios
Presider: Praise and glory to the Father of all, through the name of the Son and the Holy Spirit. We thank you that we have been deemed worthy to receive these things at your hand.
Response: Amen.
Presider: We give thanks, our Father, for the holy vine of David, your servant, which you have made known to us through Jesus, your servant.
Response: To you be the glory forever.
Presider: We give you thanks, our Father, for the life and knowledge that you have made known to us through Jesus, your servant.
Response: To you be the glory forever.
Presider: Just as this broken bread was scattered upon the mountains and then was gathered together and became one, so may your church be gathered together from the ends of the earth into your kingdom.
Response: For yours is the glory and the power through Jesus Christ forever.
The deacons will serve the Thanksgiving Meal.

Thanksgiving after the Meal

The presider will give thanks for the faith made known to us, ending with "through Jesus, your servant."
Response: To you be the glory forever.
The presider will give thanks for spiritual food and drink, ending with "we give thanks because you are mighty."
Response: To you be the glory forever.
The presider will pray for the gathering of the church, ending with "into your kingdom, which you have prepared for it."
Response: For yours is the power and the glory forever.
Presider: May grace come, and may this world pass away.
Response: Hosanna to the God of David.
Presider: If anyone is holy, let him come; if anyone is not, let him repent.

❊ A CHURCH BULLETIN FROM AD 150—CONT. ❊

Response: Maranatha! Amen.

Thanksgiving by the Prophets and Spiritual Songs
You may bring your gifts for the poor to Presbyter Demetrios during the singing. And don't forget to pray the Lord's Prayer three times every day, as is our custom.

❊ CHRISTIAN COMPOSERS PAST AND PRESENT ❊

Many composers through history have written music for the church, or churches have employed them as organists or music directors. Not all of them, perhaps, have been known to be devout. This is a short list of some who apparently were practicing Christians of one variety or another.

Composer	Lived	Country	Faith
Giovanni Pierluigi da Palestrina	1525–1594	Italy	Catholic
Tomás Luis de Victoria	1548–1611	Spain, Italy	Catholic (priest)
Heinrich Schütz	1585–1672	Germany	Lutheran
Dietrich Buxtehude	1637–1707	Germany	Lutheran
Johann Sebastian Bach	1685–1750	Germany	Lutheran
Antonio Soler	1729–1783	Spain	Catholic (priest)*
Franz Josef Haydn	1732–1809	Austria	Catholic
William Billings	1746–1800	U.S. (MA)	Congregational
Johann Friedrich Peter	1746–1813	U.S. (PA)	Moravian**
Felix Mendelssohn	1809–1847	Germany	Lutheran (had Jewish roots)
Anton Bruckner	1824–1896	Austria	Catholic
Igor Stravinsky	1882–1971	Russia, France, and U.S.	Orthodox, Catholic
Edmund Rubbra	1901–1986	England	Catholic
Lennox Berkeley	1903–1990	England	Catholic
Olivier Messiaen	1908–1992	France	Catholic
Arvo Pärt	1935–	Estonia	Orthodox
John Tavener	1944–	England	Orthodox

*Soler was a member of a religious order. Antonio Vivaldi (1678–1741) was also a priest, but he does not appear to have been especially devout.

**Peter was educated for the ministry.

❦ A TRADITIONAL EASTER VIGIL ❦

The Great Vigil of Easter is a traditional service held the night preceding Easter morning. Here is an outline of the usual order of worship. The word *Alleluia* should not occur anywhere until the time indicated below.

1. The service begins in dim light. The large paschal (Easter) candle is lit at the rear of the church, with traditional or appropriate prayer, then carried toward the front of the church. The person carrying the candle (usually a deacon) calls out, "The Light of Christ!" and the people respond, "Thanks be to God!" This occurs three times.
2. After the candle is set in place, the candle-bearer or another singer sings the traditional *Exsultet*, beginning, "Rejoice now, heavenly hosts and choirs of angels . . ."
3. A series of Scripture readings follows, setting forth the story of redemption. If not all of them are read, the passage from Exodus should not be omitted. Each reading may be followed by a selection from the Psalms (the usual choices given here) or appropriate music, followed by a suitable prayer or collect.

   a. *The Creation*—Genesis 1:1–2:2, with Psalm 33:1–11 or 36:5–10
   b. *The Flood*—Genesis 7:1–5, 11–18; 8:8–18; 9:8–13, with Psalm 46
   c. *Abraham's Sacrifice of Isaac*—Genesis 22:1–18, with Psalm 33:12–22 or Psalm 1
   d. *Israel's Deliverance at the Red Sea*—Exodus 14:10–15:1a, with Exodus 15:1b–18
   e. *God's Presence in a Renewed Israel*—Isaiah 4:2–6, with Psalm 122
   f. *Salvation Offered Freely to All*—Isaiah 55:1–11, with Isaiah 12:2–6 or Psalm 42:1–7
   g. *A New Heart and a New Spirit*—Ezekiel 36:24–28, with Psalm 42:1–7
   h. *The Valley of Dry Bones*—Ezekiel 37:1–14, with Psalm 30 or 143
   i. *The Gathering of God's People*—Zephaniah 3:12–20, with Psalm 98 or 126

4. Candidates for baptism are baptized at this time, and/or the congregation renews its baptismal vows using the words of the Apostles' Creed.
5. The leader and people then exchange the traditional Easter greeting. Before the greeting, appropriate preparatory music may be sung, and after the greeting, worshipers may ring bells.
   "Alleluia! Christ is risen!"
   "The Lord is risen indeed! Alleluia!"
6. The *Gloria in excelsis*, *Te Deum* or other triumphant hymn may be sung.
7. After prayer, the epistle is read: Romans 6:3–11, followed by Psalm 114.
8. The gospel is read: Matthew 28:1–10; Mark 16:1–8; or Luke 24:1–12.
9. A homily (short sermon) may be preached here.
10. General prayers may be offered here.
11. The service of Holy Communion (Eucharist) follows.
12. The service concludes with appropriate joyful music and the dismissal.

❧ DENOMINATIONAL AFFILIATIONS ❧
OF U.S. PRESIDENTS

George Washington . . . . Church of England (Episcopal)*
John Adams . . . . Congregational (Unitarian)**
Thomas Jefferson . . . . Episcopalian (Deist)***
James Madison . . . . Episcopalian
James Monroe . . . . Episcopalian
John Quincy Adams . . . . Congregational (Unitarian)**
Andrew Jackson . . . . Presbyterian
Martin Van Buren . . . . Dutch Reformed
William Henry Harrison . . . . Episcopalian
John Tyler . . . . Episcopalian
James Knox Polk . . . . Presbyterian
Zachary Taylor . . . . Episcopalian
Millard Fillmore . . . . Unitarian
Franklin Pierce . . . . Episcopalian
James Buchanan . . . . Presbyterian
Abraham Lincoln . . . . Raised Baptist, nondenominational
Andrew Johnson . . . . Raised Baptist, nondenominational
Ulysses S. Grant . . . . Presbyterian
Rutherford B. Hayes . . . . Methodist
James A. Garfield . . . . Disciples of Christ
Chester A. Arthur . . . . Episcopalian
Grover Cleveland . . . . Presbyterian
Benjamin Harrison . . . . Presbyterian
Grover Cleveland . . . . Presbyterian
William McKinley . . . . Methodist
Theodore Roosevelt . . . . Dutch Reformed
William Howard Taft . . . . Unitarian
Woodrow Wilson . . . . Presbyterian
Warren G. Harding . . . . Baptist
Calvin Coolidge . . . . Congregationalist
Herbert Hoover . . . . Quaker
Franklin Delano Roosevelt . . . . Episcopalian
Harry S. Truman . . . . Baptist
Dwight D. Eisenhower . . . . Presbyterian
John F. Kennedy . . . . Roman Catholic
Lyndon Baines Johnson . . . . Disciples of Christ
Richard M. Nixon . . . . Quaker
Gerald Ford . . . . Episcopalian
Jimmy Carter . . . . Southern Baptist

❊ DENOMINATIONAL AFFILIATIONS ❊
OF U.S. PRESIDENTS—CONT.

Ronald Reagan . . . . Presbyterian
George H. W. Bush. . . . . Episcopalian
William Jefferson Clinton . . . . Southern Baptist
George W. Bush . . . . Methodist

*Washington was a member of the established church in Virginia, which had been part of the Church of England before the American Revolution. The Protestant Episcopal Church was not formed until 1789, shortly after Washington was inaugurated.
**The American Unitarian Association was formed in 1825. Before that, the Orthodox and Unitarian Congregational churches of Massachusetts were not differentiated.
***Jefferson was nominally a member of the established church in Virginia, which became part of the Protestant Episcopal Church, but by belief he was a nonsupernaturalist Deist who created his own version of the Bible.

❊ WHERE THE FOUR *H*'S CAME FROM ❊

The 4-H clubs are well-known organizations for rural youth in the United States and Canada. What the *H*'s stand for is stated in the 4-H Pledge:

I pledge:
My Head to clearer thinking,
My Heart to greater loyalty,
My Hands to larger service, and
My Health to better living,
For my club, my community, my country,
and my world.

The four *H*'s go back to the description of four ways in which the young Jesus grew (Luke 2:52): "And Jesus increased in wisdom and in stature, and in favor with God and man." The parallels can be seen as follows:

Head . . . . Wisdom
Heart . . . . Favor with God
Hands . . . Favor with man
Health . . . Stature

❃ WELL-KNOWN LATIN HYMNS ❃

"All Glory, Laud, and Honor"—*Gloria, laus et honor*, Theodulph of Orleans, ninth century

"Christ Is Made the Sure Foundation"—*Angularis fundamentum*, seventh century

"All Creatures of Our God and King"—*Cantico di fratre sole*, Francis of Assisi, 1225

"Good Christian Men, Rejoice"—Attributed to Heinrich Suso (1295–1366)

"Humbly I Adore Thee"—*Adoro te devote*, Thomas Aquinas, thirteenth century

"A Hymn of Glory Let Us Sing"—*Hymnum canamus Domino*, Venerable Bede, eighth century

"Jesus, the Very Thought of Thee"—*Jesu dulcis memoria*, Bernard of Clairvaux, twelfth century

"Jesus, Thou Joy of Loving Hearts"—*Jesu dulcis memoria*, Bernard of Clairvaux, twelfth century (another translation)

"O Come, All Ye Faithful"—*Adeste fidelis*, eighteenth century

"O Come, O Come, Emmanuel"—*Veni Emanuel*, twelfth century

"O Sacred Head, Now Wounded"—*Salve caput cruentatum*, Bernard of Clairvaux, twelfth century

"O Sons and Daughters, Let Us Sing"—*O filii et filiae*, Jean Tisserand, fifteenth century

"O What Their Joy and Their Glory Must Be"—*O quanta qualia sunt illa Sabbata*, Peter Abelard, twelfth century

"The Strife Is O'er, the Battle Done"—*Finita jam sunt praelia*, twelfth century

"To Thee before the Close of Day"—*Te lucis ante terminum*, seventh century

"Unto Us a Boy Is Born"—*Puer nobis nascitur*, fifteenth century

❃ AVERAGE SIZE OF A CHURCH ❃
IN CANADA AND THE UNITED STATES

There are an estimated 350,000 churches in the United States, and an estimated 9,000 Protestant churches in Canada (not counting Catholic and other bodies).

The average attendance of churches in the United States is around 90. In Canada, evangelical churches report an average attendance of 135 and growing, while for traditional Protestant denominations the figure is 113 and declining.

Evangelical churches typically have a higher average attendance than membership, while the reverse is true of older mainline denominations. In the United States, about 45 percent of the population claims to regularly attend a church. For Canada, the figure is said to be around 20 percent.

❈ SANTA CLAUS AND OTHERS LIKE HIM ❈

Jolly old Saint Nick, a.k.a. St. Nicholas or Santa Claus, is pretty much a denizen of North America, but he has his counterparts in the Christmas visitors, gift-givers, or pranksters of many countries:

Austria	Christkind
Belgium and the Netherlands	Noël, Sinterklaas, Christkind, and Black Pete
Brazil	Papa Noel
Chile	Viejo Pascuerro
China	The Christmas Old Man (Dun Che Lao Ren)
Denmark	Julinisse
England	Father Christmas, Kriss Kringle
Finland	Old Man Christmas
France	Père Noël or le Petit
Germany	Kriss Kringle, Christkind, or St. Nicholas
Hawaii	Kanakaloka
Italy	Befana
Japan	Santa Kurohsu
Mexico	The Three Kings
Poland	The Star Man or Wise Men
Russia	Babushka, a grandmother figure
Spain	The Three Kings
Sweden	Jultomten or the Christmas Brownie, and the Christmas goat (*julbok*)

❈ THE SEVEN SORROWS OF THE VIRGIN MARY ❈

A traditional Catholic list of events that brought sorrow to Jesus' mother:

1. The prophecy of Simeon, that "a sword will pierce through your own soul also" (Luke 2:35)
2. The flight into Egypt to escape from Herod (Matt. 2:13–14)
3. Losing Jesus while returning from the feast in Jerusalem (Luke 2:42–45)
4. Meeting Jesus on the way to Calvary (perhaps based on Luke 23:27–28)
5. Standing at the foot of the cross (John 19:26)
6. When Jesus was taken down from the cross (Luke 23:53)
7. Jesus' entombment (John 19:41–42)

❄ WORLD RELIGIONS AT THEIR CORE ❄

There are many ways of stating the principles at the core of Christian faith. Here is one attempt to do so, in order to compare Christianity with other major world religions. Notice that only in Christianity is the core of faith bound up with a relationship to a particular person, instead of following certain practices.

Christianity

1. God created all things to glorify him.
2. Sin, or disregard for God's purpose, separates people from God and destroys life.
3. God works through history, especially through a people he calls, to restore his purpose.
4. God has realized his renewal of creation in the life, death, and resurrection of Jesus.
5. God brings people into the life of his renewed creation through their membership in Christ.

Judaism

Judaism would accept the first three points of Christianity, described above, perhaps stated differently.

Islam (the "Five Pillars")

1. God (Allah) is One, and Muhammad is his authoritative spokesman.
2. A cycle of daily prayers is the duty of every worshiper.
3. Believers are obligated to help the needy.
4. Worshipers of Allah are to purify themselves through fasting.
5. All who are able must make a pilgrimage to Mecca.

Buddhism (the "Noble Truths")

1. Life is full of grief and suffering.
2. Suffering arises from attachment to desires.
3. Ridding yourself of desire brings an end to suffering.
4. The "Eightfold Path" brings freedom from suffering: right outlook, thought, speech, action, livelihood, effort, mindfulness, and contemplation.

Hinduism

1. God is manifested in many gods such as Brahma (creator), Vishnu (sustainer), Shiva (destroyer), Krishna, Ganesha, and others.
2. *Avatars* are incarnations of the gods, becoming gods themselves—hence Hinduism's many gods.
3. The *Vedas*, *Upanishads*, and other sacred writings are reverenced.
4. Certain principles govern life, including:

❋ WORLD RELIGIONS AT THEIR CORE—CONT. ❋

a. *karma*—a soul's particular quality, good or bad
b. *reincarnation*—The soul is reborn in another form based on its *karma*; hence all life is sacred.
c. *dharma*—various moral and religious laws
d. *maya*—Final truth is illusory. Hinduism, therefore, has wide diversity of belief and practice and absorbs ideas from other religions.

❋ THE OLDEST MANUSCRIPTS ❋
OF THE NEW TESTAMENT

The oldest fragments of the New Testament were written on *papyrus*, an early paper made from reeds. Later manuscripts, called *codices* (singular *codex*), were in book form and used *vellum*, sheets made from the skin of lambs, kids, or calves. The New Testament was not written on scrolls, as were the separate books of the Hebrew Scriptures. In scholarly practice, papyri were numbered and preceded with *P*. The oldest codices, called *uncials* because they were written in capital letters only, were symbolized by letters (there is an alternate numbering scheme).

Manuscript	Symbol	Contents	Date
John Rylands Papyrus	P 52	Part of John 18	Around AD 150
Chester Beatty Papyri	P	Fragments of Gospels, Acts, and Epistles	Around 200
Bodmer Papyri	P	Parts of Luke and John, the Epistles of Peter and Jude	Third century AD
Codex Vaticanus	B	Complete Greek Bible	Fourth century AD
Codex Sinaiticus	?	Complete Greek Bible	Fourth century AD
Codex Alexandrinus	A	Most of the Greek Bible	Around AD 500
Codex Ephraemi rescriptus	C	Most of the Greek Bible	Fifth century AD
Codex Bezae	D	Gospels and Acts, both Greek and Latin	Fifth or sixth centuries AD
Codex Claromontanus	D_2	Epistles of Paul	Sixth century AD

BIBLICAL WEIGHTS AND MEASURES

OLD TESTAMENT

Weight

gerah (1/20 shekel)	0.6 gram
beka (1/2 shekel)	1/5 ounce
pim (2/3 shekel)	1/4 ounce
shekel	2/5 ounce
mina, 50 shekels	1 1/4 pounds
talent, 3,000 shekels	75 1/2 pounds

Length, Distance, and Area

finger	7/10 inch
handbreadth (4 fingers)	3 inches
span (2 handbreadths)	8 3/4 inches
cubit (6 handbreadths)	17 1/2 inches
pace	length of a step
semed (yoke)	5/8 acre

Capacity, Dry

kab	1 1/5 quarts
omer (1/10 ephah)	2 quarts
seah (1/3 ephah)	2/3 peck
ephah	1/2 bushel
lethech (1/2 homer)	2 1/2 bushels
homer, cor	5 1/5 bushels

Capacity, Liquid

log	2/3 pint
hin	1 gallon
bath	5 1/2 gallons
cor, homer	55 gallons

NEW TESTAMENT

Weight

talent	a large weight
pound	12 ounces

Length, Distance, and Area

fathom	6 feet
stadion (furlong)	1/8 mile
milion (mile)	9/10 mile

Capacity, Dry

modios (bushel)	1/4 bushel

Capacity, Liquid

metretes (firkin)	10 gallons
litra (pound)	12 ounces

THE FOUR CHIEF ARCHANGELS

Archangel	*Name Means*	*Reference*	*Feast Day (West)*
Michael	"Who is like God?"	Daniel 10, 12; Jude; Revelation 12	September 29
Gabriel	"Man of God"	Daniel 8, 9; Luke 1	March 24
Raphael	"God has healed"	Books of Tobit and Enoch (Apocryphal)	October 24
Uriel	"God is my light"	Book of Enoch (Apocryphal)	July 28

❧ POPULAR SAINTS ❧

Which saints have been the most popular among Roman Catholics in North America? One good indication is how many churches have been named after them. A survey of twenty major cities in Canada and the United States yielded the following, in order of frequency. More than one saint held some of these names, but we have described the most likely possibility. This list does not include the twelve disciples or the apostle Paul, also often called *Saint* by Protestants.

Patrick . . . . Missionary to Ireland, fifth century
Michael . . . . Archangel, mentioned in Daniel, Jude, and Revelation
Anthony . . . . Founder of monastic movement, fourth century
Ann . . . . Traditionally the mother of the Virgin Mary
but not mentioned in the Bible
Bernadette . . . . Her visions of the Virgin Mary gave
rise to healing pilgrimages to Lourdes, France
Theresa . . . . Spanish mystic, sixteenth century
George . . . . Legendary early Christian martyr, patron saint of England
Augustine . . . . Theologian, fifth century
Nicholas . . . . Pope, ninth century
Cecelia . . . . Legendary early Christian martyr, patron saint of music
Helena . . . . Mother of the Roman emperor Constantine,
third to fourth century
Catherine . . . . Visionary, fourteenth century

❧ DANTE'S LEVELS OF HELL ❧

Dante Alighieri (1265–1321), in his *Inferno* (part of the *Divine Comedy* trilogy), developed a picture of nine layers, or rings, of hell:

1. Limbo, the place of virtuous non-Christians and unbaptized children
2. The Lustful, those who sinned in the flesh
3. The Gluttonous, who lived with excess
4. The Avaricious and Prodigal, who lived greedily and wastefully
5. The Wrathful and Gloomy, who lived lives of crudity and vindictiveness
6. Heretics, who refused to believe in God or the afterlife
7. The Suicides, who committed violence against God and nature
8. Malebolge, abode of various types of the fraudulent and malicious
9. Cocytus, the lowest level where Satan, the Arch Traitor, eternally chews the bodies of Judas and other betrayers

❄ FAMOUS MISSIONARIES ❄

Some well-known Christian missionaries since the 1500s.

Missionary	Lived	Nationality	Missionary to
Francis Xavier	1506–1552	Navarre (Spain)	Japan, China
Jacques Marquette	1636–1675	France	American Indians, Great Lakes region
David Brainerd	1718–1747	Connecticut (Colonial America)	American Indians in Middle Colonies
Junipero Serra	1713–1784	Spain, Mexico	American Indians in California
William Carey	1761–1834	England	India
Samuel Marsden	1764–1838	England	Australia, New Zealand
Adoniram Judson	1788–1850	United States	Burma
John Geddie	1815–1872	Canada	Eastern Melanesia, South Pacific
David Livingstone	1813–1873	Scotland	Southern Africa
Robert Moffatt	1795–1883	Scotland	South Africa
Alexander Mackay	1849–1890	Scotland	Uganda
James Chalmers	1841–1901	Scotland	Cook Islands, New Guinea
Hudson Taylor	1832–1905	England	China
George Grenfell	1849–1906	England	Congo
Mary Slessor	1848–1915	Scotland	Nigeria, Benin
Solomon Ginsburg	1867–1927	Poland/ England	Brazil
Charles T. Studd	1860–1931	England	China, India, Africa
Jonathan Goforth	1859–1936	Canada	China
Jim Elliot	1927–1956	United States	Ecuador
Albert Schweitzer	1875–1965	Alsace (Germany/ France)	French Equatorial Africa
Gladys Aylward	1900–1970	England	China

❄ FIVE PHILISTINE CITIES ❄

The Philistines, who gave the Israelites so much grief after their settlement in Canaan, also gave their name to the land we now call *Palestine*. Their five main cities, located in what is now called the *Gaza Strip*, were Ashkelon, Ashdod, Ekron, Gath, and Gaza.

✼ THE ORIGIN OF CHAPTERS AND VERSES ✼

The Bible originally had no chapter or verse references. When people referred to portions of Scripture, they used subject matter or first words as a title.

Stephen Langton, archbishop of Canterbury, divided the Latin Bible into chapters in 1205 to make it easier to cite biblical texts. Scholars working with Cardinal Hugo de Santo Care made a chapter division around 1248. The practice spread to other languages, with the chapters divided into lettered sections, usually seven. Rabbi Nathan printed a Hebrew Bible with verse divisions in Venice in 1524. Robert Estienne (Stephanus, or Stevens) of Paris, a Protestant, introduced numbered verses in his printed editions of the Greek New Testament in 1551 and the Hebrew Bible in 1571. The Geneva Bible of 1560 was the first English Bible with both chapter and verse numbers.

In the English Bible, there are 594 chapters before Psalm 118 and 594 chapters after Psalm 118; 594 plus 594 equals 1,188. Psalm 118:8 says, "It is better to take refuge in the LORD / than to put confidence in man."

✼ MUSICAL INSTRUMENTS OF THE BIBLE ✼

Instrument	Selected References	Comments
Cymbal	1 Chronicles 15:16 (NASB); Psalm 150:5 (KJV)	Several types; evidently there was a difference between "loud cymbals" and "high sounding cymbals"
Gong	1 Corinthians 13:1 (NASB)	Mentioned by Paul; used in pagan temples
Harp	Psalm 150:3 (NASB); Revelation 5:8 (NASB)	Usually an instrument of ten strings
Horn	Joshua 6:5 (NLT); Psalm 81:3	Ram's horn (*shofar, qeren, yobel*) used for signaling
Lyre	Psalm 43:4 (NASB); Isaiah 5:12 (NASB)	Several types, some of them mentioned among Nebuchadnezzar's instruments (Dan. 3)
Pipe	Psalm 150:4 (NASB); Luke 7:32 (KJV)	A reed flute, associated with both rejoicing and mourning
Sistrum	2 Samuel 6:5 (NKJV)	A rattle-like instrument
Tambourine	Exodus 15:20 (NLT); Psalm 68:25 (NASB)	Typically played by women, associated with dance
Trumpet	Numbers 10:8–10 (NASB)	Of silver, used similarly to the ram's horn

❊ THE FAMOUS LAMBETH QUADRILATERAL ❊

The Lambeth Conferences are periodic gatherings of the bishops of all the churches in the worldwide Anglican Communion. They are held at Lambeth Palace, the London residence of the archbishop of Canterbury. The 1888 conference put forth the Anglican view of the essentials for the reunification of the Christian church in four articles known as the *Lambeth Quadrilateral*. They are also called the *Chicago Lambeth Articles*, having originated in the 1886 General Convention of the Protestant Episcopal Church in Chicago.

1. The Holy Scriptures of the Old and New Testaments, "containing all things necessary to salvation," are the ultimate standard of faith.
2. The Apostles' Creed is the baptismal symbol, and the Nicene Creed is the sufficient statement of Christian faith.
3. Baptism and the Lord's Supper, which Christ ordained, are the two sacraments.
4. The office of bishop, adapted to local conditions (the *historic episcopate*), is the focal point for the unity of the church.

❊ THE NICENE CREED ❊

The Nicene Creed, or Niceno-Constantinopolitan Creed, is thought to have been enlarged from the statement of the Council of Nicaea (325) after the Council of Constantinople (381).

We believe in one God, the Father, the Almighty, maker of heaven and earth, of all that is, seen and unseen.

We believe in one Lord, Jesus Christ, the only Son of God, eternally begotten of the Father, God from God, Light from Light, true God from true God, begotten, not made, of one Being with the Father. Through him all things were made. For us and for our salvation he came down from heaven: by the power of the Holy Spirit he became incarnate from the Virgin Mary, and was made man. For our sake he was crucified under Pontius Pilate; he suffered death and was buried. On the third day he rose again in accordance with the Scriptures; he ascended into heaven and is seated at the right hand of the Father. He will come again in glory to judge the living and the dead, and his kingdom will have no end.

We believe in the Holy Spirit, the Lord, the giver of life, who proceeds from the Father and the Son. With the Father and the Son he is worshiped and glorified. He has spoken through the Prophets. We believe in one holy catholic and apostolic Church. We acknowledge one baptism for the forgiveness of sins. We look for the resurrection of the dead, and the life of the world to come. Amen. (Book of Common Prayer, 1979)

❦ WHO REFORMED THE REFORMATION? ❦

Martin Luther's break with Rome may seem a radical enough step, but others in the sixteenth century wanted to go even farther than Luther, Calvin, Zwingli, or the other "standard" Reformers. Today the term *Anabaptist* is generally applied to members of this "radical Reformation." It refers to people who rebaptize because they do not recognize the validity of baptism in the established churches—whether Catholic or Reformed—which they considered corrupt. But the radical reformers were concerned with more than baptism. They had several major beliefs:

1. The church must be restored to its primitive form, with no links to the state.
2. The Scriptures are the supreme authority in matters of faith. Other Reformers believed this, but the radicals applied the principle more consistently.
3. Infant baptism has no basis in Scripture, hence the practice of rebaptizing converts.
4. The Lutheran doctrine of justification by faith alone does not have enough foundation in Scripture; a holy life separated from the corruptions of society is also necessary for salvation.
5. Both church and civil society must be rebuilt according to the principles of the kingdom of God; for some of these reformers, this meant forming communities of shared life and resources similar to the communist ideal.
6. Some communities held a heightened expectation of the imminent return of Christ.

Both the Catholic Church and the major Reformers denounced and persecuted leaders of various groups in this radical reform movement, and as a result many of their followers eventually found their way to North America. Their spiritual descendants today are the Mennonites, Amish, Hutterites, and similar groups, and many of their beliefs have had a lasting influence on the thinking and practice of Baptists, Quakers, and the evangelical churches in general.

❦ JESUS GOES TO HOLLYWOOD: ❦ MOVIES ABOUT THE LIFE OF CHRIST

A few of these films would not be thought consistent with a Christian viewpoint.

The Robe (1953) • *King of Kings* (1927, 1961) • *The Greatest Story Ever Told* (1965)
Jesus Christ Superstar (1973) • *Jesus of Nazareth* (1977) • *Jesus* (1979)
The Last Temptation of Christ (1988) • *The Gospel of John* (2003)
The Passion of the Christ (2004)

❧ WOMEN WHO LED THE ISRAELITES ❧

Miriam—Prophetess, sister of Moses and Aaron. She led a celebration after the Exodus (Exod. 15:20) and later a protest against Moses' authority (Num. 12:1).

Deborah—She was a prophetess who judged Israel (Judg. 4:4).

Jael—She killed the Canaanite general Sisera (Judg. 4:21).

Bathsheba—Wife of David and mother of Solomon. She convinced the aged David to name her son his successor in place of the expected Adonijah (1 Kings 1:15–18).

Athaliah—Queen of Judah. She ruled as a usurper between the death of her son Ahaziah and the coronation of the boy Joash (2 Kings 11:1–3).

Huldah—Prophetess. She encouraged King Josiah to reform worship according to the rediscovered Book of the Law (2 Kings 22:14–20).

Esther—Queen of Persia. She convinced King Ahasuerus to let the Jews protect themselves and established the customs of Purim (Esther 9:25–32).

Judith—Widow of Bethulia. She killed the invading general Holofernes and encouraged the Jews to throw off his army.

The Queen Mother—Bathsheba and Athaliah. She seems to have played an important role in the life of Judah. The Bible often gives the names of the mothers of the kings, and the king mentions the Queen Mother (in the phrase "son of thy handmaid" in Pss. 86 and 116). Catholic theologians sometimes justify the veneration of the Virgin Mary, mother of Jesus Christ, on the basis of the Queen Mother's role.

❧ BALD AND FAT MEN OF THE BIBLE ❧

Eglon, king of Moab, was "a very fat man" (Judg. 3:17). Eli, the priest, was "an old man, and heavy" (1 Sam. 4:18).

Elisha was called "baldhead" by some boys (2 Kings 2:23). Perhaps, as a prophet, he was tonsured like a monk and the boys were actually belittling him as a man of God. (After they finished taunting Elisha, the boys were mauled by two bears.)

Paul, the apostle, may have been bald. The apocryphal Acts of Paul describes him as "a man little of stature, thin-haired upon the head, crooked in the legs, of good state of body, with eyebrows joining, and nose somewhat hooked."

Paul

❧ BIBLE MONEY IN TODAY'S DOLLARS ❧

In the Old Testament, the *shekel* is a unit of weight in silver. Thus people could use it for money. At recent rates for silver, it would be worth about $2.50 today. Abraham paid Ephron the Hittite 400 shekels of silver for land to bury his wife, Sarah, or $1,000 in current North American value. A *talent* was 3,000 shekels, or about $7,500. A gold talent would be worth $476,400 U.S.

In the New Testament world, both Greek and Roman coins were in use. One mentioned often in the New Testament is the Roman *denarius*. It was one twelve-hour-day's wage for a day laborer (Matt. 20:9–10). Based on current U.S. and Canadian minimum-wage laws, that would be about $72, not counting overtime. But a better comparison would be Palestinians working in Israel, for whom a day's wage is about $19 U.S. The Greek *drachma* was worth about the same as a denarius.

Other New Testament coins can be valued in relation to the denarius, using the Palestinian rate, as follows:

Lepton (mite, Jewish coin) . . . . . Worth about the same as the following but required for a contribution to the temple, which would not accept Greek or Roman coinage because a Gentile ruler's head was stamped on it.

Quadrans (farthing, Roman) . . . ¼₄ denarius, 29 cents. The widow's contribution to the temple treasury (Mark 12:42) was about 58 cents.

Assarius (farthing, Roman) . . . . . ⅟₆ denarius, $1.19, the price of two sparrows (Matt. 10:29).

Stater (Greek) . . . . 4 denarii, $76, the tax Peter was to pay for Jesus and himself (Matt. 17:27).

❧ THE ORIGINS OF EASTER ❧

Easter is the oldest festival of the Christian church, perhaps going back to the second century. Its origin as a feast is found in the Jewish Passover, since Jesus' resurrection took place in connection with the Passover celebration.

The early medieval church was marked by the *Paschal controversies*, bitter disputes over how to determine the date of the Easter celebration. In the Western church Easter can fall anywhere from March 21 through April 25, depending on the date of the Paschal full moon.

The link between Easter and Passover has been important in Christian theology and worship. As Passover celebrates the exodus of the Israelites from Egyptian slavery, Easter celebrates the new "exodus" of Christ and his own from sin and death to new life.

❀ ENGLISH BIBLE TRANSLATIONS, POPULAR, ❀ HISTORIC, AND OBSCURE

These are some of the historic or widely used translations of the complete Bible, out of the approximately five hundred translations of the Old and New Testaments that have been produced. Several important Jewish translations that include only the Hebrew Scriptures are not included, nor are New Testament–only versions.

1380s . . . . John Wycliffe—Completed by John Purvey

1525 . . . . William Tyndale—First printed English Bible

1560 . . . . Geneva Bible—First English Bible with numbered verses

1610 . . . . Douay-Rheims Bible—Catholic, from Latin

1611 . . . . Authorized Version (King James)

1881 . . . . Revised Version—England

1901 . . . . American Standard Version

1926 . . . . The Bible: A New Translation by James Moffatt, England

1952 . . . . Revised Standard Version

1955 . . . . The Holy Bible: A Translation from the Latin Vulgate—
Catholic, by Ronald Knox

1960 . . . . Confraternity Edition—Catholic, from Latin

1961 . . . . New English Bible

1965 . . . . The Amplified Bible

1966 . . . . Jerusalem Bible—Catholic

1970 . . New American Bible—first Catholic English Bible from the original languages

1971 . . . . New American Standard Bible

1971 . . . . The Living Bible—paraphrase by Kenneth Taylor

1976 . . . . Today's English Version (Good News)—by Robert Bratcher

1978 . . . . New International Version

1982 . . . . New King James Version

1985 . . . . New Jerusalem Bible—Catholic

1986 . . . . International Children's Bible

1987 . . . . New Century Version

1990 . . . . New Revised Standard Version

1992 . . . . Revised English Bible—revision of New English Bible

1996 . . . . Contemporary English Version—revision of Today's English Version

1996 . . . . New Living Translation

2002 . . . . English Standard Version—revision of Revised Standard Version

❧ ENGLISH BIBLE TRANSLATIONS, POPULAR, ❧ HISTORIC, AND OBSCURE—CONT.

Some Unusual Translations

1808 .... The Holy Bible, Containing the Old and
New Covenant—first English translation of the
Septuagint (Greek Old Testament), by Charles Thomson,
secretary of the Continental Congress

1867 .... The Holy Scriptures, Translated and Corrected by
the Spirit of Revelation—adaptation of King James
Version by Joseph Smith, with Mormon emendations;
published after his death

1903 .... The Holy Bible in Modern English—
by Ferrar Fenton, a businessman and amateur translator

1957 .... The Holy Bible from Ancient Eastern
Manuscripts—by George M. Lamsa, based on Syriac Peshitta version

1960 .... New World Translation—Jehovah's Witnesses

❧ THE LITURGICAL COLOR SCHEME ❧

Many churches change the color of altar and pulpit hangings (sometimes called *ante-pendia*) or clergy garb (stoles and other vestments) depending on the seasons and days of the liturgical calendar. The following is a typical scheme for Western churches.

Advent .... Violet or Blue (sometimes Rose for
the third Sunday, called *Gaudete*)
Christmas .... White
Epiphany Day .... White
Epiphany Season .... Green
Palm Sunday and Holy Week .... Red
Good Friday, Holy Saturday .... Black, or altar is bare
Easter and Ascension .... White
Pentecost .... Red
Pentecost Season .... Green*
Trinity Sunday .... White
All Saints' Day .... White
Christ the King .... White

*Green, the "neutral color," is typically used during "ordinary time," the period between Pentecost and Advent.

❈ BAPTIST GROUPS IN NORTH AMERICA ❈

Fifty-one Baptist fellowships or associations are organized in the United States and Canada.

Alliance of Baptists

American Baptist Association

American Baptist Churches in the USA

Association of Reformed Baptist Churches of America

Association of Regular Baptist Churches (Canada)

Baptist Bible Fellowship International

Baptist General Conference

Baptist General Conference of Canada

Canadian Baptist Ministries

Canadian Convention of Southern Baptists

Central Baptist Association

Conservative Baptist Association of America

Continental Baptist Churches

Convention of Atlantic Baptist Churches

Cooperative Baptist Fellowship

Evangelical Free Baptist Church

Fellowship of Evangelical Baptist Churches in Canada

Full Gospel Baptist Church Fellowship

Fundamental Baptist Fellowship Association

Fundamental Baptist Fellowship of America

General Association of Baptists (Duck River Baptists)

General Association of General Baptists

Global Independent Baptist Fellowship

Independent Baptist Fellowship of North America

Independent Baptist Network

Institutional Missionary Baptist Conference of America

L'Association des Églises Missionnaire Baptiste Landmark du Québec

Liberty Baptist Fellowship

National Association of Free Will Baptist Churches

National Baptist Convention of America, Inc.

National Missionary Baptist Convention of America

New England Evangelical Baptist Fellowship

New Testament Association of Independent Baptist Churches

North American Baptist Conference

Original Free Will Baptist Convention

Primitive Baptist Church

Progressive National Baptist Church

Separate Baptists in Christ

Southern Baptist Convention

Seventh Day Baptist General Conference

Sovereign Grace Landmark Independent Baptist Churches

Two-Seed-in-the-Spirit Predestinarian Baptists

Ukranian Evangelical Baptist Convention of Canada

United American Free Will Baptist Church

United American Free Will Baptist Conference

World Baptist Fellowship

❉ HEBREW-ARAMAIC WORDS WE STILL USE TODAY ❉

Some words used in English are derived from Hebrew, the language of most of the Old Testament, and its sister language, Aramaic, which the Jews spoke during the New Testament period. A few proper names also seem to be derived from Hebrew. This list includes some terms in addition to the more obviously theological words, such as *amen, hallelujah, messiah, Pharisee, rabbi,* and *Satan.*

abbey, abbot .... An abbey is a monastic community governed by an abbot, from *abba,* "father."

alphabet .... From *aleph* and *beth,* the first two letters of the Hebrew alphabet

behemoth .... A large creature (Job 40:15), perhaps the origin of the name of the Bahamas

cabal .... An intrigue, from *qabbalah,* "secret lore"

cherub .... A small angel, and by extension a pleasant little child, from paintings by Michelangelo; but originally the cherubim were the much more fearsome guardian figures with the ark of the covenant

Europe .... From *erev,* "evening." Europe was the land of the setting sun for the ancient Hebrews and Phoenicians.

gauze .... From the city of Gaza

hosanna .... An exclamation of joy, from the cry "Save us, we beseech thee" (Ps. 118:25).

jubilee .... A celebration, especially a fifty-year anniversary, from *yobel,* the ram's horn blown to signal the Year of Jubilee (Lev. 25:9)

leviathan .... A large creature or sea monster (Ps. 104:26, et al.)

sabbath, sabbatical ..... The seventh day or a period of rest from normal activity, as in a faculty member's sabbatical year, from the Hebrew *shabbat,* based on the word for the number seven

scallion .... A type of onion, from the city of Ashkelon

seraph .... A member of a traditional order of angels, from the Hebrew plural *seraphim,* "burning ones" (see Isa. 6:2)

shibboleth .... A belief or motto that defines who belongs to one's party or group. The Hebrew word has no relevant meaning but was used in an intra-Israelite feud to filter out men from the other side who could not pronounce it correctly (Judg. 12:5–6).

sodomy .... The practice of homosexual behavior, from the city of Sodom (Gen. 19:4–5)

❦ SUPERSCRIPTIONS IN THE PSALMS ❦

About half of the psalms have introductory notes, or *superscriptions*. These notes may indicate the type of psalm, the collection to which it belongs, instructions for performance (the instruments used and perhaps the name of a tune), an event in the life of David to which the psalm relates, or the name of another who composed the psalm. Here are some of the superscriptions, as given in the Revised Standard Version.

Psalm	Superscription
3	A Psalm of David, when he fled from Absalom his son.
5	To the choirmaster: for the flutes. A Psalm of David.
7	A Shiggaion of David, which he sang to the LORD concerning Cush a Benjaminite.
16	A Miktam of David.
17	A Prayer of David.
18	To the choirmaster. A Psalm of David the servant of the LORD, who addressed the words of this song to the LORD on the day when the LORD delivered him from the hand of all his enemies, and from the hand of Saul. He said:
34	A Psalm of David, when he feigned madness before Abimelech, so that he drove him out, and he went away.
45	To the choirmaster: according to Lilies. A Maskil of the Sons of Korah; a love song.
50	A Psalm of Asaph.
51	To the choirmaster. A Psalm of David, when Nathan the prophet came to him, after he had gone in to Bathsheba.
56	To the choirmaster: according to The Dove on Far-off Terebinths. A Miktam of David, when the Philistines seized him in Gath.
60	To the choirmaster: according to Shushan Eduth. A Miktam of David; for instruction; when he strove with Aram-naharaim and with Aram-zobah, and when Joab on his return killed twelve thousand of Edom in the Valley of Salt.
67	To the choirmaster: with stringed instruments. A Psalm. A Song.
72	A Psalm of Solomon.
75	To the choirmaster: according to Do Not Destroy. A Psalm of Asaph. A Song.
90	A Prayer of Moses, the man of God.
100	A Psalm for the thank offering.
145	A Song of Praise.* Of David.

*The title of the book of Psalms in Hebrew is *tehillim*, "Praises," but only Psalm 145 is called a "praise" in its superscription. The English title "Psalm" is a translation of Hebrew *mizmor*, a piece sung to the accompaniment of a stringed instrument.

❄ CHRISTIANS WHO LIVE IN COMMUNES ❄

The early Christians in Jerusalem "were together and had all things in common" (Acts 2:44). Since apostolic times, groups of Christians have tried communal living. There have been, and still are, communes with a distinctly Christian orientation as well. The following is a partial list.

The Munster commune of the 1530s comprised an entire Dutch city taken over by a radical Anabaptist movement; a Catholic army destroyed it.

The Hutterites of Canada and the northwestern United States form one of the oldest and largest communal systems. They originated as a German-speaking Anabaptist group in central Europe, and after moving to Russia, emigrated to America in the late 1800s.

Herrnhut was the Moravian-Pietist commune Count Nikolaus Zinzendorf established and led in Saxony in 1927. The Moravians were influential in the life of John Wesley.

The Shakers, or United Society of Believers in Christ's Second Coming, were founded in England by Mother Ann Lee in 1758. Their nickname came from their enthusiastic movements, or dancing, during worship. They spread to the American colonies and became famous for their handcrafts. They were celibate, and only a handful remain in a Maine community.

The Harmony Society, or Rappites, was a German pietist group of the 1800s in Pennsylvania and Indiana. The community was known for the quality of its textile and other manufacturing. Partly due to the practice of celibacy, it declined and disbanded in 1905.

Bethany Fellowship, an evangelical community in the Minneapolis area, was founded in 1945. It trains and supports missionaries and recently sold its Christian publishing house.

Jesus People USA is a communal group in Chicago famous for its association with the former Rez Band (the Resurrection Band, which was formed by Glen Kaiser in 1971). The community has become a member congregation of the Evangelical Covenant Church.

Reba Place Fellowship is a community in Evanston, Illinois, associated with Reba Place Church, a member of the Illinois Mennonite Conference.

❄ ARAMAIC PASSAGES OF THE BIBLE ❄

Many Christians know the Old Testament was written in Hebrew and the New Testament in Greek. What is not so well known is that a few parts of the canonical Old Testament are written in Aramaic, a language the Jews spoke after the Babylonian exile. It is also called *Chaldee*, after Chaldea, an old name for Babylonia. The Bible passages in Aramaic are Ezra 4:8–6:18; Ezra 7:12–26; and Daniel 2:4–7:28.

❊ STATIONS OF THE CROSS ❊

One aspect of Christian worship is to reenact and take part in events of the life of Christ. Outstanding examples of this are the Lord's Supper, "following the Lord in baptism," and processions on Palm Sunday. Worshipers in many Catholic and Anglican churches also pray around the Stations of the Cross during Lent or Holy Week, passing by a series of carvings or icons (pictures) depicting Jesus' journey toward the tomb. A few of the events, such as the appearance of Veronica, are legendary. The "stations" are often arranged around the outer walls of the church's worship space.

Pilate condemns Jesus to death	Jesus tells the women of Jerusalem not to weep for him.
Jesus receives his cross	Jesus falls a third time.
Jesus falls under the cross	Jesus is stripped of his clothing.
Jesus meets his mother	Jesus is nailed to the cross.
Simon of Cyrene takes up the cross	Jesus dies on the cross.
Veronica wipes the face of Jesus	Jesus' body is taken down from the cross.
Jesus falls a second time	Jesus' body is placed in the tomb.

❊ SOME CHRISTIAN "OLATRIES" ❊

The suffix *-olatry* is derived from the Greek verb *latreuo*, meaning "I worship." Any kind of false worship might be labeled an "olatry."

Angelolatry . . . . Veneration of angels

Bibliolatry . . . . Bible worship; making a particular interpretation of the Bible more important than Jesus Christ as a criterion of faith

Ecclesiolatry . . . . Obsession with church traditions in the place of devotion to Christ

Hagiolatry . . . . Worship of saints

Hierolatry . . . . Worship of saints or sacred things

Idolatry . . . . Worship of idols; any excessive preoccupation with values other than God

Mariolatry . . . . Veneration of the Virgin Mary to the point of worship, or substituting her for Jesus

❊ BIRDS HAVE NESTS, ❊ FOXES HAVE DENS, CLERGY HAVE . . .

Many Protestant churches do not maintain homes for their clergy, preferring to include a housing allowance as part of their compensation. Others, however, still provide such housing. Catholic priests, having taken a vow of poverty, own little property and must live in what the church provides. Some of the terms used for clergy housing:

Parsonage—Many Protestant churches
Rectory—Catholic, Episcopal, Church of England
Manse—Presbyterian, Lutheran
Vicarage—Church of England
Episcopal Residence—Methodist bishops
Palace—Old term for the residence of an Anglican or Catholic bishop, one still used for Lambeth Palace, the London residence of the archbishop of Canterbury

❊ COUNTRIES WITH THE MOST ANGLICANS ❊

The Church of England is the established church in England, claiming between 27 and 33 million adherents. However, only around 9 million have been confirmed, and the number of those regularly receiving Holy Communion on Easter Sunday is estimated at between 1,700,000 and 2,800,000. Out of 70 million nominal Anglicans in the world, more than half (53 percent) live in the developing world, 35 million of them in Africa alone. The most Anglican country in the world is Nigeria, whose 17.5 million adherents make up 14 percent of the total population. There are 8 million Anglicans in Uganda. The Episcopal Church in the USA, the largest Anglican body in North America, is about 14 percent of the size of the Church of Nigeria and less than 1 percent of the total population of the United States.

❊ MOST POPULAR NAMES FOR THE POPE ❊

John	24*	Pius	12
Gregory	16	Stephen	10
Benedict	15	Boniface	9
Clement	14	Alexander	8
Innocent	13	Urban	8
Leo	13		

*There were two popes John XXIII. The first is considered an "antipope" and is normally not counted. Other splinter group antipopes have taken some of these names.

❊ TYPES OF CHRISTIAN CHORAL MUSIC ❊

Anthem . . . . In the broad sense, a choral piece with religious lyrics usually sung only by a choir

Antiphon . . . . A piece sung responsively by two different groups, or the response in such a piece (see *Verse*)

Cantata . . . . A composition of choral or solo "numbers" usually based on one seasonal theme or the lessons appointed for a certain day of the church year

Chant . . . . A nonmeasured* setting of a biblical or liturgical text, usually sung in unison and unaccompanied

Chorale . . . . A hymn usually sung in a slower, statelier manner

Gospel Song . . . . A measured* song with stanzas, sung by a congregation; it differs from the hymn in focusing on the singer's faith rather than God, the object of faith

Hymn . . . . The term commonly applied to any measured song, with stanzas, sung by a congregation

Mass . . . . A setting of the Catholic Mass (those portions not said by the priest nor varying with the calendar)

Motet . . . . Similar to an anthem but usually with many interweaving parts and unaccompanied

Oratorio . . . . A composition of both choral and solo "numbers," more extended than a cantata and usually based on a biblical theme, character, or story

Psalm . . . . There are several forms of psalm singing; see separate entry.

Refrain . . . . A portion of a song repeated after each stanza; also called *chorus*

Requiem . . . . A composition commemorating the dead, usually a setting of the Requiem Mass

Stanza . . . . That part of a song repeated with the same music but different words; often erroneously called *verse*

Verse . . . . The part of a responsive song that varies each time, while the antiphon remains the same; also applied to stanza

Worship Chorus . . . . A song sung by the congregation in a more "contemporary" style than the traditional hymn or gospel song; also called *praise chorus*

Measured means having a regular beat and bar lines.

❦ THE ATHANASIAN CREED ❦

The Athanasian Creed, or *Quicunque Vult*, from its opening words in Latin, is traditionally ascribed to Athanasius (296–373) but is of a later time. It is seldom used in
worship today.

*Whosoever will be saved, before all things it is necessary that he hold the catholic
faith; which faith except every one do keep whole and undefiled, without doubt he
shall perish everlastingly. And the catholic faith is this: That we worship one God
in Trinity, and Trinity in Unity; neither confounding the persons nor dividing the
substance. For there is one person of the Father, another of the Son, and another of
the Holy Spirit. But the Godhead of the Father, of the Son, and of the Holy Spirit
is all one, the glory equal, the majesty coeternal. Such as the Father is, such is the
Son, and such is the Holy Spirit. The Father uncreated, the Son uncreated, and the
Holy Spirit uncreated. The Father incomprehensible, the Son incomprehensible,
and the Holy Spirit incomprehensible. The Father eternal, the Son eternal, and the
Holy Spirit eternal. And yet they are not three eternals but one eternal. As also there
are not three uncreated nor three incomprehensible, but one uncreated and one
incomprehensible.*

*So likewise the Father is almighty, the Son almighty, and the Holy Spirit
almighty. And yet they are not three almighties, but one almighty. So the Father is
God, the Son is God, and the Holy Spirit is God; and yet they are not three Gods,
but one God. So likewise the Father is Lord, the Son Lord, and the Holy Spirit
Lord; and yet they are not three Lords but one Lord. For like as we are compelled
by the Christian verity to acknowledge every Person by himself to be God and
Lord; so are we forbidden by the catholic religion to say; There are three Gods or
three Lords.*

*The Father is made of none, neither created nor begotten. The Son is of the
Father alone; not made nor created, but begotten. The Holy Spirit is of the Father
and of the Son; neither made, nor created, nor begotten, but proceeding. So there
is one Father, not three Fathers; one Son, not three Sons; one Holy Spirit, not three
Holy Spirits. And in this Trinity none is afore or after another; none is greater or
less than another. But the whole three persons are coeternal, and coequal. So that
in all things, as aforesaid, the Unity in Trinity and the Trinity in Unity is to be
worshipped. He therefore that will be saved must thus think of the Trinity.*

*Furthermore it is necessary to everlasting salvation that he also believe rightly
the incarnation of our Lord Jesus Christ. For the right faith is that we believe and
confess that our Lord Jesus Christ, the Son of God, is God and man. God of the
substance of the Father, begotten before the worlds; and man of substance of His
mother, born in the world. Perfect God and perfect man, of a reasonable soul and
human flesh subsisting. Equal to the Father as touching His Godhead, and inferior
to the Father as touching His manhood. Who, although He is God and man, yet*

❃ THE ATHANASIAN CREED—CONT. ❃

He is not two, but one Christ. One, not by conversion of the Godhead into flesh, but by taking of that manhood into God. One altogether, not by confusion of substance, but by unity of person.

For as the reasonable soul and flesh is one man, so God and man is one Christ; who suffered for our salvation, descended into hell, rose again the third day from the dead; He ascended into heaven, He sits on the right hand of the Father, God, Almighty; from thence He shall come to judge the quick and the dead. At whose coming all men shall rise again with their bodies; and shall give account of their own works. And they that have done good shall go into life everlasting and they that have done evil into everlasting fire. This is the catholic faith, which except a man believe faithfully he cannot be saved.

❃ CLIMBING THE CHURCH LADDER: ❃ LEVELS OF HOLY ORDERS

In addition to the roles of apostle, evangelist, prophet, and pastor-teacher, the New Testament mentions deacons ("servers"), presbyters ("elders"), and bishops ("overseers") as functionaries in the church. Various Christian groups handle these distinctions in different ways. This is a sketch.

In many evangelical churches, those designated as deacons and elders are laypeople. Pastors are elders, too, but are not usually so called.

In some churches, elders can be either lay or clergy. Presbyterians have both "ruling elders" (lay) and "teaching elders" (clergy, now often called *ministers of word and sacrament*). The "Christian" churches and some others have "preaching elder" as their ministerial title.

In Methodist churches, people are ordained deacons as a steppingstone toward full ordination as an elder. A bishop is an elder who has been *consecrated* (not *ordained*) to preside over an area or conference.

In Anglican, Catholic, or Orthodox churches, the deaconate (deacons) and priesthood are levels of Holy Orders for the ministry. (The term *priest* is derived from *presbyter*.) Bishops are a third order of ordination; Catholic and Orthodox theology holds that the fullness of the church resides in the office of the bishop. In these churches are also permanent deacons who perform certain roles in the church and are not on a path toward the priesthood.

In virtually all Christian groups, ordination to the offices of deacon, elder (priest), or bishop is done through the laying on of hands and prayer according to the model of Acts 13:3. The Catholic church formerly recognized several "minor orders" of subdeacon, acolyte, exorcist, reader, and doorkeeper, but they are now suppressed as orders and laypersons usually perform their remaining functions.

❊ AFRICANS IN THE BIBLE ❊

Moses' wife, a Cushite ... Num. 12:1 ...... Cush was the region south of Egypt (modern Sudan and Ethiopia), but there was a Cush in Asia as well. Moses' wife, Zipporah, was a Midianite, so either the Cushite wife was a second wife or Cush was another name for Midian, not in Africa.

The Queen of Sheba .... 1 Kings 10:1–5 ... Sheba, who was highly impressed with Solomon, was traditionally equated with Ethiopia, but modern authorities locate it in the southern part of the Arabian Peninsula near modern Yemen.

The Ethiopians .... Amos 9:7 .... In this passage, Amos quoted God: "'Are you not like the Ethiopians to me, / O people of Israel?' says the LORD. / 'Did I not bring up Israel from the land of Egypt, / and the Philistines from Caphtor / and the Syrians from Kir?'" His point was that the Lord is involved in the affairs of other peoples, including those from Africa.

Simon of Cyrene .... Mark 15:21 ..... Simon carried Jesus' cross. Cyrene was modern Libya; people from Cyrene were also present on the Day of Pentecost (Acts 2:10).

The Ethiopian eunuch .. Acts 8:27 .... According to this verse, the eunuch was "a minister of Candace, queen of the Ethiopians." Unless he was a prose-lyte like Nicolaus of Antioch, one of the first deacons (Acts 6:5), this official is the first non-Jewish convert to Christianity mentioned after the Resurrection.

Simeon called Niger .... Acts 13:1 .... Simeon was a prophet in Antioch. *Niger* means "black" (from Latin, but in the Greek text), but whether this Simeon was a black African or simply a dark-skinned Mediterranean is im-possible to tell.

❀ TITLES OF CHURCH WORKERS ❀
WHO AREN'T PASTORS OR PRIESTS

Everyone is familiar with clergy titles, such as *minister*, *pastor*, or *priest*, and a number of others. The titles of *elder* and *deacon* are used for both clergy and laypeople. Here are some titles for *nonclergy* functionaries in the church.

Acolyte . . . . Person, often young, who lights the altar candles and serves at the altar in other ways

Altar boy (girl) . . . . A young person who assists the presiding clergy with the vessels of Holy Communion or performs other altar duties

Beadle . . . . Official appointed to care for the place of worship; in some early New England churches, the beadle carried a pole with which to awaken dozing worshipers

Cantor . . . . Singer who leads a responsorial psalm or other music

Chorister . . . . Member of a choir

Clerk . . . . Person assigned to record actions by a church board (vestry, session) or to record baptisms and marriages. The word *clerk* is derived from *cleric*, as is the word *clergy*.

Crucifer . . . . Person who carries the cross in a procession

Lector . . . . A person who reads a Scripture lesson; also simply called Reader

Minister . . . . When used of laypeople, it often refers to liturgical assistants such as Communion ministers, prayer ministers, or ministers of music.

Precentor . . . . Person appointed to lead singing

Sexton . . . . Originally, the official responsible for maintaining church property, including vestments, books, and sacramental vessels, or placed in charge of the church cemetery or ringing the church bell; now sometimes another term for the janitor. The word comes from the Latin *sacrista*.

Steward . . . . A term formerly applied to members of the board of a Methodist church

Superintendent . . . . Term often applied to the head of a Sunday school and, of course, used for many other types of church officials

Torchbearer . . . . Person, often young, who carries candles in a procession

Trustee . . . . Member of the board responsible for making decisions about church property. In some cases, the trustees are the legal owners of the property.

❀ TITLES OF CHURCH WORKERS ❀
WHO AREN'T PASTORS OR PRIESTS—CONT.

Usher . . . . Person responsible for seating worshipers, distributing materials, or collecting the offering

Verger . . . . Official assigned to keep order in a service, or to lead a procession or reader to the proper place; carries a baton called a *verge* (you saw them in the National Cathedral during President Reagan's funeral)

❀ COMPARATIVE HEIGHT OF BIBLICAL MOUNTAINS ❀

Mount Ararat	16,900	Mount Zion	2,533
(in modern Turkey)			
Mount Lebanon	10,000	Mount Nebo*	2,500
Mount Hermon	9,230	Mount Moriah	2,430
Mount Sinai (*Jabal Musa*)	7,500	Mount Tabor	1,930
Mount Ebal	3,080	Mount Carmel	1,700
Mount Gerizim	2,850	Mount Gilboa	1,700
Mount of Olives	2,690	Mount of Jesus' Temptation	1,148

Elevations are approximate feet above sea level.

*Mount Nebo rises 3,850 feet above the surface of the Dead Sea, which is 1,350 feet below sea level.

❀ RELIGION AND VOTING ❀

A survey following the 2000 presidential election in the United States revealed a link between politics and participation in religious organizations. Almost two-thirds of voters who attended religious services at least once a week voted for the Republican candidate, while two-thirds of those who seldom attend church services voted for the Democratic ticket. The survey did not identify the religious groups, but it would seem that voters in conservative or evangelical groups would be more likely to be frequent church attendees, while those in more mainline or "liberal" groups might be, on the average, less active.

❧ SOME PRESIDENTS OF THE ❧ NATIONAL ASSOCIATION OF EVANGELICALS

1942–44 .... Harold J. Ockenga (Presbyterian)

1946–48 .... Rutherford L. Decker (Southern Baptist)

1948–50 .... Stephen W. Paine (Wesleyan Methodist)

1958–60 .... Herbert S. Mekeel (Presbyterian USA)

1962–64 .... Robert A. Cook (Evangelical Free)

1968–70 .... Arnold Oldon (Evangelical Free)

1978–80 .... Carl H. Lundquist (Baptist General Conference)

1982–84 .... Arthur E. Gay Jr. (Conservative Congregational)

1984–86 .... Robert W. McIntyre (Wesleyan)

1988–90 .... John H. White (Reformed Presbyterian)

1990–92 .... B. Edgar Johnson (Nazarene)

1992–95 .... David Rambo (Christian and Missionary Alliance)

1995–98 .... Don Argue (Assemblies of God)

1999–2001 .... Kevin Mannoia (Free Methodist)

2002–03 .... Leith Anderson, Interim (Baptist General Conference)

Current .... Ted Haggard (Southern Baptist/Nondenominational)

❧ TYPES OF CHURCH GOVERNMENT ❧

Who decides the major (and minor) issues affecting the life of a church? Christians have struggled over this question as much as over any theological issue. Advocates for four historic forms of church government have all claimed the New Testament church's practice as the basis for their views:

1. Episcopal—Responsibility for the church rests with a bishop (Greek *episkopos*, "overseer") within a particular region. Examples: Roman Catholic, Greek Orthodox, Anglican/Episcopal.

2. Presbyterial—The local church receives direction from a body of presbyters (from Greek for "elders") from its sister churches. Examples: Presbyterian, United Methodist, Lutheran.

3. Congregational—The local church governs itself, ultimately through a congregational meeting. Examples: Baptist, Congregational, Churches of Christ ("Christian").

4. Monarchical—Decisions are made by the local pastor. Examples: many Pentecostal churches.

❦ CHRISTIAN SYMBOLS ❦

Hand of God
God the Father

Triumphant Lamb
Victorious Christ

Descending Dove
Holy Spirit

Trefoil
The Holy Trinity

Celtic Cross

Ship
The Church

Purse and Coins
Jesus' Betrayal by Judas

Chalice and Wafer
The Eucharist

Alpha-Omega
Monogram
Jesus, the Beginning
and the End

Chi Rho
First Two Letters of
"Christ" in Greek

Cross and Globe
(Orb)
Christ's Worldwide
Dominion

Latin Cross

Greek Cross

Jerusalem Cross

Russian or
Eastern Cross

Maltese Cross

❄ THE ROSARY ❄

The rosary is a series of prayers developed during the Middle Ages that Catholics use to venerate the Virgin Mary and seek her help.

The rosary beads form a circle with an extension ending in a crucifix. The circle is divided into five decades (groups of ten), each marked off by a larger or more separated bead, and the extension has five beads—two large or separated, with three others between them. The entire rosary, when recited, consists of twenty decades, or four circles, of the beads. Each circle of recitation contemplates five "mysteries" of Christ and the Virgin Mary. Traditionally there were three groups of mysteries: the Joyful, the Sorrowful, and the Glorious. Pope John Paul II added the Luminous Mysteries in 2002. As an example, the five Glorious Mysteries are the resurrection of Jesus, his ascension, the descent of the Holy Spirit, Mary's assumption into heaven, and her coronation as Queen of Heaven and Earth.

A standard procedure for praying the rosary:

1. Holding the crucifix, make the sign of the cross, and recite the Apostles' Creed.
2. Pray the "Our Father" (Lord's Prayer) on the first large bead.
3. Say a "Hail Mary" for an increase of faith, hope, and charity on each of the next three beads: "Hail Mary, full of grace; the Lord is with thee: blessed art thou among women, and blessed is the fruit of thy womb, Jesus. Holy Mary, Mother of God, pray for us sinners, now and at the hour of our death. Amen."
4. Recite the Gloria Patri on the next large bead: "Glory be to the Father, and to the Son, and to the Holy Ghost. As it was in the beginning, is now, and ever shall be, world without end. Amen."
5. Say the "Fatima Prayer": "My Jesus, forgive us our sins, save us from the fires of hell, and lead all souls to heaven, especially those in most need of thy mercy."
6. Contemplate the first Mystery (a mystery about Christ or the Virgin Mary, e.g., the resurrection of Jesus) in the first group, and pray the Our Father on the large bead.
7. On each of the next ten small beads ("decade"), recite a Hail Mary while reflecting on the Mystery.
8. On the next large bead, recite the Gloria Patri and the Fatima Prayer.
9. Continue in the same manner with the other four Mysteries on the following decades, until the circuit is complete.

❈ COMPARING THE THREE JEWISH ❈ TEMPLES OF THE BIBLE

The Israelite-Jewish sanctuary on Mount Zion in Jerusalem is commonly called the *temple*, but the Old Testament usually calls it the "house of the Lord" (Hebrew *bet-Yahweh*) or "house of God" (*bet-'Elohim*). It was built three times.

Solomon's Temple

The temple of Solomon was completed around 960 BC. The architect, Hiram, was a Phoenician, and the temple in many ways resembled sanctuaries outside Israel. First Kings 5–8 describe its construction and dedication. During David's reign the sanctuary (the tabernacle or tent) had been in Gibeon. Nebuchadnezzar, king of Babylon, destroyed Jerusalem and its temple in 587 BC.

The "Second Temple"

The book of Ezra records events surrounding the rebuilding of the temple. The community of returned exiles from Babylon, apparently led by the prince Zerubbabel, completed it around 515 BC. Little is known about this temple, but it stood for almost five hundred years, longer than either of the other two.

Herod's Temple

Herod (called "the Great") was an Idumean, whose people had been forcibly converted to Judaism. In 37 BC he managed to get himself appointed ruler of Judea by the Romans, who controlled the area. He was unpopular with his subjects and began the rebuilding of the temple in part to win their favor. It was a far more magnificent structure than the first two temples, and it took more than eighty years to complete. Construction began around 20 BC and was going on during the ministry of Jesus, who foretold its end (Mark 13:1–2). Shortly after its completion in AD 63, Herod's temple was destroyed in the Jewish revolt of AD 66–70.

Reconstruction of Herod's Temple

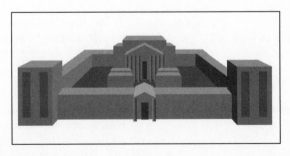

❋ BISHOPS AND THEIR JURISDICTIONS ❋

The word *bishop* comes from the Greek *episkopos*, which means "overseer" or "superintendent." In the New Testament it seems to refer to the man who had chief oversight for the church in a certain location. Today various Christian or historically related groups use the term *bishop* in different ways. This list indicates some of the typical jurisdictions, or areas of responsibility, bishops hold in several major groups in North America.

Group	*Jurisdiction*	*Comments*
African Methodist Episcopal	Episcopal District	
African Methodist, Episcopal Zion	Episcopal District	
Anglican (various groups including "continuing"* and missionary churches)	Diocese	Missionary bishops may work where a diocese has not yet been organized, as in the Anglican Mission in America.
Charismatic Episcopal Church	Diocese	Never part of Episcopal Church; new group formed in 1992
Christian Methodist Episcopal Church	Episcopal District	Predominantly African-American group
Church of Jesus Christ of Latter Day Saints (Mormon)	Ward	A ward is a local Mormon congregation.
Episcopal Church in the United States of America	Diocese	
Evangelical Lutheran Church in America	Synod (regional)	
Missionary Baptist	Local Church	An African-American group
Pentecostal/ Charismatic churches (various)	Local Church	African-American congregations are more likely to call their pastors "Bishop," but the practice exists among other groups also.
Reformed Episcopal Church	Diocese	Established in 1873
Roman Catholic Church	Diocese	In the U.S. the diocese is incorporated as the bishop. The man holding the office legally owns all

✤ BISHOPS AND THEIR JURISDICTIONS—CONT. ✤

Group	Jurisdiction	Comments
		church properties within his diocese except those belonging to religious orders or other nondiocesan Catholic organizations.
United Methodist Church	Area	An area consists of one or more regional Annual Conferences.

*A "continuing" Anglican church is a body that has formed to continue established worship practices and doctrinal standards modified by the Episcopal Church in the United States or the Anglican Church of Canada.

✤ WHY THE HUGUENOT DID FRANCE NEVER BECOME PROTESTANT? ✤

John Calvin (Jean Cauvin), the Protestant Reformer, was French, so why did France never become Protestant? Actually the Reformation spread rapidly through France despite persecution, and many of the nobility became Protestants. They came to be called *Huguenots*, a name of uncertain origin though it may be a corruption of the German term *Eidgenossen*, "confederates." Civil war and assassinations broke out between militant Catholics, Protestants, and a third group that simply wanted political order. The St. Bartholomew's Day massacre of 1572 took the life of the Huguenot leader Admiral Gaspard de Coligny, among others.

After Henry of Navarre, originally a Protestant, became king of France, he issued the Edict of Nantes in 1598, which gave the Huguenots the right to live securely in their fortified towns. Louis XIV (reigned 1643–1715), however, revoked the edict in 1685 and the persecution of Protestants resumed. About three hundred thousand Huguenots made their way to the Netherlands, Switzerland, Germany, England, Ireland, America, and eventually South Africa. In the American colonies they founded French-speaking churches, most of which eventually merged into the Presbyterians after French ceased to be spoken.

After the Enlightenment and the Revolution, religious persecution diminished in France and the spiritual descendants of the Huguenots remain a small, but often influential, community. Maurice Couve de Murville, French foreign minister (1958–1968) was a member of the Reformed Church. The Oratory of the Louvre, across the street from the famed art museum of Paris, is a Reformed "temple" or church; a statue of Admiral Coligny stands in the courtyard. The only French Calvinist congregation in the United States is the Huguenot Church of Charleston, South Carolina; founded in 1687, it has not had an unbroken history but was reestablished in 1983.

❧ LIFESTYLES OF MONKS, ❧
HISTORIC AND CONTEMPORARY

Cenobites . . . . This term refers in general to monks who live in a monastic community, but there are many variations of such life. Some cenobites live similarly to hermits, having solitary cells but within a common building or enclosure. They may observe a rule of silence, such as the famous Trappists, except during the community worship. Other monastic communities follow a less-strict rule.

Cloistered . . . . A cloister is an enclosed area, originally an arcade linking the building of a cathedral complex. Today the term *cloister* refers to the house of a religious order, but the term *cloistered* refers in particular to monastics who never leave their building or compound.

Discalceds . . . . Monastic orders whose members do not wear shoes are called *discalced*, from a Latin word meaning "shoeless." Originally these monks went barefoot (Francis of Assisi is an example), but today they wear sandals.

Hermits . . . . A hermit withdraws to a solitary life, often in a cave and sometimes in a loose community with other hermits. This "eremitic" life was popular among devoted Christians from the third century till the Middle Ages.

Anchorites . . . . These persons withdrew to a solitary life of silence, prayer, and deprivation. Eventually they came to be enclosed in walled-up cells, sometimes attached to churches. Julian of Norwich (1342–1413) was a female anchorite.

Stylites . . . . Simeon Stylites (390–459) lived in solitude on top of a pillar (Greek *stylos*) near Antioch, gradually increasing its height to sixty feet until his death. Other stylites followed his example during the fifth through tenth centuries and afterward.

❧ U.S. CITIES WITH THE MOST ❧
CHRISTIAN ORGANIZATIONS

By telephone directory listings, there are 108 Christian ministries, organizations, and publishers in greater Orlando, Florida; 54 in Colorado Springs, Colorado; and 28 in and around Wheaton or Carol Stream, Illinois. This does not count local churches or Christian educational institutions.

❄ THE CHIEF END OF MAN, ACCORDING ❄ TO THE WESTMINSTER CONFESSION

Question: What is the chief and highest end of man?
Answer: Man's chief and highest end is to glorify God, and fully to enjoy him forever.

A certain Catholic catechism contains a similar statement:

> The desire for God is written in the human heart, because man is created by God and for God; and God never ceases to draw man to himself. Only in God will he find the truth and happiness he never stops searching for.

❄ RAILROAD CHAPEL CARS ❄

Several churches and missionary organizations operated railroad chapel cars in the western United States from 1890 through the 1940s. The cars were pulled by regular passenger or freight trains and set out on sidings along railway lines. By means of these cars, missionaries and priests were able to preach and administer the sacraments in remote or newly settled areas, and they reportedly founded churches in more than three thousand locations.

The Episcopal Church operated three cars. The first was the Cathedral Car of North Dakota Church of the Advent, which the Pullman Company of Chicago built in 1890. The Episcopal Diocese of Northern Michigan operated two additional cars converted from existing railway rolling stock.

Baptist chapel cars traveled throughout the West beginning in 1891. Evangel was the first car the American Baptist Publication Society operated, followed by Emmanuel, Glad Tidings, Good Will, Messenger of Peace, and Herald of Hope. The last Baptist car, Grace, was dedicated in 1915 and is displayed today at Green Lake, Wisconsin. Smith and Barney of Dayton, Ohio, built most of the Baptist cars.

The Catholic Extension Society had three chapel cars: St. Anthony, St. Peter, and St. Paul. The first was dedicated in 1907, a wooden Wagner Palace car reconditioned by the Pullman Company; the other two were steel. The St. Paul apparently served until 1954.

❄ SATAN: REAL OR IMAGINED? ❄

In 1990, 55 percent of the American public believed the devil to be real. Five years later:
70 percent believed in the devil   10 percent weren't sure
19 percent did not believe in the devil 1 percent had no opinion

❄ MOST-REPEATED WORDS IN THE BIBLE ❄

Some words appear quite often in the English Bible. The frequency of their occurrence could suggest some of the Bible's major concerns.

Say, says, said, saying .... 6,915 times in 6,446 verses
Come, comes, came, coming .... 3,633 times in 3,496 verses
Go, goes, went, gone, going .... 3,367 times in 3,120 verses
Give, gives, gave, given, giving .... 2,202 times in 2,093 verses
Life, live, lives, lived, living .... 1,406 times in 1,254 verses
Word, words .... 1,216 times in 1,170 verses
Hear, hears, heard, hearing .... 1,199 times in 1,145 verses
Speak, speaks, spoke, spoken, speaking .... 994 times in 966 verses
Death, die, dies, died, dying .... 975 times in 870 verses
Right, righteous, righteousness .... 921 times in 872 verses
Call, calls, called, calling .... 840 times in 805 verses
Heart, hearts .... 837 times in 783 verses
Sin, sins, sinned, sinning, sinner, sinners .... 813 times in 743 verses
Love, loves, loved, loving .... 706 times in 642 verses
Kill, kills, killed, killing, slay, slays, slain, slew, slaying .... 695 times in 665 verses
Child, children .... 621 times in 553 verses
Work, works, worked, working .... 585 times in 545 verses
Bless, blesses, blessed, blessing .... 500 times in 470 verses
Wife, wives .... 493 times in 452 verses
Faith, faithful, faithfulness .... 417 times in 397 verses
Glory, glories, glorify, glorified, glorifies .... 415 times in 387 verses
Salvation, save, saves, saved, saving .... 407 times in 398 verses
Peace, peaceful .... 367 times in 338 verses
Pray, prays, prayer, prayed, praying .... 303 times in 389 verses
Praise, praises, praised, praising .... 284 times in 253 verses
Believe, believes, believed, believing, believer, believers ... 281 times in 265 verses
Soul, souls .... 243 times in 230 verses
Judge, judged, judging .... 195 times in 178 verses
Grace, gracious .... 181 times in 171 verses
Witness, witnesses .... 181 times in 169 verses
Steadfast love or loving-kindness .... 177 times in 175 verses
    (Hebrew *hesed*, "covenant love")
Mercy, mercies, merciful .... 160 times in 153 verses
Obey, obeys, obeyed, obeying .... 141 times in 137 verses
Trust, trusts, trusted, trusting .... 112 times in 111 verses

❊ CZAR NICHOLAS II—SAINT AND MARTYR ❊

Russian revolutionaries executed Czar Nicholas II and his family, the Romanovs, in 1918 at Ekaterinburg in Siberia. Following the demise of the Soviet Union, their remains were discovered and were reburied in 1998 in the Tomb of the Czars in St. Petersburg. In 2000, the Russian Orthodox Church declared the czar and his family official saints and martyrs. The declaration called them "people who sincerely sought to live by the commandments of the Gospel" and stated that in their humble endurance of suffering, "the evil-defeating light of the faith of Christ was revealed."

❊ DAYS OF THE WEEK ❊

The days of the week in the English language owe their names to ancient Greek and Roman practice, as carried through the Germanic peoples. The Greeks named the days of the week after the sun, the moon, and the five known planets, which were in turn named after the gods Ares, Hermes, Zeus, Aphrodite, and Cronus. The Romans substituted their equivalent gods for those of the Greeks: Mars, Mercury, Jupiter, Venus, and Saturn. The second through seventh days in Latin-derived languages such as French retain the Roman names: *lundi* (Luna, the moon), *mardi, mercredi, jeudi, vendredi, samedi*. The Germanic peoples substituted similar gods for the Roman ones for these days (except Saturday), resulting in the names of our days:

> Sunday (the sun)
> Monday (the moon)
> Tuesday (Tiu, equivalent to Ares and Mars)
> Wednesday (Woden, equivalent to Hermes and Mercury)
> Thursday (Thor, equivalent to Zeus and Jupiter)
> Friday (Freya, equivalent to Aphrodite and Venus)
> Saturday (Cronus, Saturn)

In the Latin-derived languages, however, Sunday is not named after the sun, but after the Lord (Latin *dominus*), as in Spanish *domingo*, French *dimanche*.

In modern Hebrew the days of the week are simply numbered, as in *yom rishon*, "first day," and so on through *shabbat* (seventh).

❧ FAMOUS PHYSICALLY DISABLED ❧ OR HANDICAPPED CHRISTIANS

This short list does not include people who became disabled as a result of a final illness.

The apostle Paul was harassed by a "thorn in the flesh" (2 Cor. 12:7 KJV). Some interpreters have suggested he had a vision problem, based on Galatians 4:15 and 6:11.

Origen of Alexandria, early Christian theologian, castrated himself.

Teresa of Avila had a severe illness that left her legs paralyzed for three years (she eventually improved).

Fanny Crosby, the hymn writer, was blind from infancy.

Helen Keller (died 1968) became both blind and deaf due to illness at the age of nineteen months.

Harold Wilke (died 2003), a United Church of Christ minister and founder of the National Organization on Disability, was born without arms.

The Ethiopian official whom Philip converted was rendered a eunuch (Acts 8:27).

Peter Abelard, medieval theologian, was castrated by thugs sent by the uncle of his lover, Héloïse.

John Milton, the Puritan writer, was blind for the last twenty-three years of his life.

William Seymour, pioneer of the Pentecostal revival of the early 1900s, was blinded in one eye by smallpox while in his twenties.

Ken Medema, Christian concert artist and music therapist, has been blind from birth.

Joni Eareckson Tada, Christian writer and speaker, became a quadriplegic in a diving accident as a young woman.

❧ THE WESLEY GRACE ❧

John Wesley composed a "grace" to be prayed before meals. It is usually sung to the tune "Old Hundredth," familiar to many Protestants as the doxology.

> Be present at our table, Lord;
> Be here, and everywhere, adored.
> These mercies* bless, and grant that we
> May feast in fellowship* with thee.

*Wesley's original words were "creatures" and "paradise."

❈ FIRST BIBLES OFF THE PRINTING PRESS ❈

Johann Gutenberg (1398–1468) is regarded as the inventor of printing in Europe. Johann Fust and Peter Schoeffer took over Gutenberg's printing operation in Mainz, Germany, in 1455; the following year, they published the Gutenberg Bible as their first printed book.

The next three Bibles published were the 1462 Bible printed in Mainz by Fust and Schoeffer, on vellum with illustrations (forty-nine copies are known); the 36-Line Bible, so called because it has thirty-six lines per page, printed in Bamberg in or before 1460 (only fourteen copies remain); and the Mentelin Bible, printed in Strasbourg in 1460 (twenty-seven copies survive). All of these first Bibles were printed in Latin.

The first Bible printed in English was William Tyndale's translation of the New Testament, printed in Germany in 1525. Possessing it was punishable by death in England, and only two copies of its first printing are known to have survived. Building on Tyndale's work, Miles Coverdale printed the first complete Bible in English in 1535, partly based on Luther's German Bible.

John Rogers printed Matthew's Bible, probably in the Netherlands, in 1537. It was an edition of the work of Tyndale and Coverdale and was the first English Bible authorized in England, though not for use in churches. Henry VIII and archbishop Thomas Cranmer authorized the Great Bible for church use; first published in 1539, it was essentially a revision of Matthew's Bible and was reprinted seven times.

The first complete English Bible translated entirely from the original languages was the Geneva Bible of 1560, which set a standard for scholarship and was reprinted as late as 1644. Though used in Scotland, it was not acceptable to English authorities because of its notes and comments, and the Bishop's Bible of 1568 was printed as a substitute. Finally the Authorized Version of 1611, known as the King James, superseded all previous English Bibles in Protestant usage.

The first Bible printed in the American colonies was in the Algonquin language; translated by the missionary John Eliot, it was printed in 1663. The first English Bible printed in America was a 1782 edition of the Authorized Version printed in Philadelphia by Robert Aitken.

❈ TEN WORDS OR PHRASES ❈
NOT FOUND IN THE BIBLE

This may surprise some folks, but these words and phrases just can't be found in the Bible.

Accepting Christ • Glossolalia (a term for speaking in tongues) • Personal Savior • Going to heaven • Inerrancy • Infallibility • Second Coming • Eternal security • Theology • Trinity

❈ SAINTS NAMED CATHERINE ❈

Name	Lived	Original Name	Nationality	Canonized
Catherine of Alexandria	d. 305		Alexandria (Egypt)	Legendary
Catherine of Siena	1347–1380	Catherine di Benincasa	Italy	1461
Catherine of Sweden (Catherine Vastanensis)	1331–1381	Catherine Gudmarsson	Sweden	1484
Catherine of Bologna	1413–1463	Catherine de' Vigri	Italy	1712
Catherine of Genoa	1447–1510	Caterina Fieschi Adorno	Italy	1737
Catherine del Ricci	1522–1590	Alessandra Lucrezia Romola	Italy	1746
Catherine of Palma	1533–1574	Catalina Tomas	Spain	1930
Catherine Labouré	1806–1876	Catherine Labouré	France	1947
Catherine Vincentia Gerosa	1784–1847	Catherine Gerosa	Italy	1950
Katherine Drexel	1858–1955	Katherine Drexel	United States	2000

Future Saints Catherine?

Name	Lived	Original Name	Nationality	Canonized
Catherine Cosie (Osanna of Cattaro)	1493–1565	Catherine Kosic	Montenegro	Beatified 1934
	1656–1680	Catherine Tekakwitha	Native American (Algonquin/Mohawk)	Beatified 1980
	d. 1794	Catherine Cottenceau	France	Beatified 1984
	d. 1794	Catherine du Verdier de la Sorinière	France	Beatified 1984
	1754–1836	Catherine Jarrige	France	Beatified 1996
	1801–1857	Caterina Cittadini	Italy	Beatified 2001
	1839–1894	Caterina Volpicelli	Italy	Beatified 2001
Catalina de Maria	1823–1896	Saturnina Rodriguez	Argentina	Beatification Pending

❧ THE SEVEN CONTRARY VIRTUES ❧

These are derived from the poem "Psychomachia" ("Battle for the Soul") by Prudentius, around 410. The virtues are the antidotes for the corresponding Seven Deadly Sins.

1. Humility	3. Abstinence	5. Patience	7. Diligence
2. Kindness	4. Chastity	6. Liberality	

❧ POPULAR HYMNS OF FANNY CROSBY ❧

Frances Jane Van Alstyne (1823–1915), known by her maiden name as Fanny J. Crosby, lost her sight at six weeks of age. She began writing poetry as a child. She became a pupil, then teacher, at the New York City Institution for the Blind. In 1858 she married the blind musician Alexander Van Alstyne. Beginning in 1864, she published more than two thousand hymns, many of them under almost one hundred other names because publishers were embarrassed by the quantity of her output. She is said to have written more than eight thousand hymns or, more correctly, "devotional lyrics." Purists do not consider her work to be of high poetic quality, but the simplicity and earnestness of her verse have endeared her songs to Christian worshipers in North America. These are some of her most-used hymns.

"All the Way My Savior Leads Me" (1875)
"Blessed Assurance, Jesus Is Mine" (1873)
"I Am Thine, O Lord" ("Draw Me Nearer," 1875)
"Jesus Is Tenderly Calling" (1883)
"Jesus, Keep Me Near the Cross" (1869)
"Pass Me Not, O Gentle Savior" (1868)
"Praise Him, Praise Him" (1869)
"Redeemed, How I Love to Proclaim It!" (1882)
"Rescue the Perishing" (1869)
"Safe in the Arms of Jesus"
"Saved by Grace" (1891)
"Savior, More Than Life to Me" (1875)
"Take the World, but Give Me Jesus" (1879)
"Tell Me the Story of Jesus" (1880)
"Thou My Everlasting Portion" ("Close to Thee," 1874)
"Though Your Sins Be as Scarlet" (1887)
"To God Be the Glory" (1875)
"Trusting Jesus" (1877)
"Watch and Pray" (1885)

❧ U.S. REVIVALS ❧

Revival	Approximate Dates	Focal Location	Major Figures
Dutch Reformed Revival	1720s	Raritan Valley, New Jersey	Theodorus J. Frelinghuysen
Log College Revival	1730–1760	Middle Colonies	Gilbert Tennent
Great Awakening	1734–1760	Western Massachusetts, spreading through eastern seaboard	Jonathan Edwards, George Whitefield
Yale Revival	1801	New Haven, Connecticut	Timothy Dwight
Frontier Revival	1801 and following	Cane Ridge, Kentucky, and throughout frontier	Barton W. Stone
Second Great Awakening	1820–1835	Western New York, spreading through northern states	Charles Grandison Finney, Lyman Beecher
Holiness Movement	1835–1910	New York City, spreading through North America	Phoebe Palmer, Charles Cullis
Pentecostal Revival	1901	Topeka, Kansas, and Los Angeles, spreading through North America	Charles F. Parham, William J. Seymour
Latter Rain Revival	1948	North Battleford, Saskatchewan; Detroit; spreading through North America	George Hawtin, Myrtle D. Beall
Wheaton College Revival	1950	Wheaton, Illinois	V. Raymond Edman
Jesus Movement	1967	West Coast, spreading throughout North America	Ted Wise, Arthur Blessit, Tony and Susan Alamo

❊ BIBLE MEN NAMED JOSHUA ❊

At least seventeen men in the Bible had a variation of the name Joshua. The full Hebrew name of Joshua is *Yehoshua'*. The name is derived from the Hebrew word meaning "salvation" or "deliverance." A variant of the name is *Yeshua'*. The Greek form of this name is *Iesous*, or Jesus. A shorter form is *Hoshea'* (same as Hosea).

1. Joshua (Hoshea), son of Nun, successor to Moses
2. Joshua of Beth-shemesh, on whose land the ark halted (1 Sam. 6:14)
3. Hoshea, son of Azaziah, an Ephraimite chief under David (1 Chron. 27:20)
4. Joshua, governor of Jerusalem under King Josiah (2 Kings 23:8)
5. Hosea, son of Beeri, the prophet
6. Hoshea, son of Elah, king of Israel
7. Hoshaiah, father of the commander Azariah (Jer. 42:1)
8. Jeshua, a Levite in the time of King Hezekiah (2 Chron. 31:15)
9. Jeshua, a Levite (Ezra 2:40)
10. Jeshua, father of Ezer (Neh. 3:19)
11. Jeshua, son of Kadmiel, a Levite (Neh. 12:24)
12. Hoshea, one of the "chiefs of the people" (Neh. 10:23)
13. Hoshaiah, a prince of Judah (Neh. 12:32)
14. Joshua, high priest in the time of the prophet Zechariah (Zech. 3:1)
15. Jesus of Nazareth
16. Jesus Barabbas*
17. Jesus called Justus, a Jewish worker with Paul (Col. 4:11)

*Several ancient manuscripts of the New Testament support the possibility that Barabbas's name was Jesus Barabbas.

❊ OTHER FAMILY TRAGEDIES ❊ EXPERIENCED BY MARTIN LUTHER KING SR.

The assassination of Dr. Martin Luther King Jr. on April 4, 1968, was a blow to all Americans, but especially to his father, the Reverend Martin Luther King Sr., pastor of Ebenezer Baptist Church in Atlanta, Georgia. But in July 1969, his other son and copastor, the Reverend A. D. Williams King, drowned in a pool accident. Then on June 30, 1974, the senior King's wife, Alberta Williams King, was shot while playing the organ in Ebenezer Baptist Church. "How much can a man take?" he asked, but at her funeral he said, "I cannot hate any man." Martin Luther King Sr. died November 11, 1984, at age eighty-four.

Incidentally, Martin Luther King Jr. was originally named Michael Luther King, but later his father changed both of their names to Martin.

❈ LEAST POPULAR BIBLICAL NAMES ❈

Girls' Names

Hoglah (Josh. 17:3)—Not very complimentary unless you think swine are beautiful

Jezebel (1 Kings 19:2)—Sort of like naming your son Hitler

Lo-Ruhamah (Hos. 1:6 NIV)—Means "not pitied"

Zillah (Gen. 4:23)—Not a bad name, but what if she marries . . . see *Gog*

Zipporah (Exod. 2:21)—Moses' wife. People might think your daughter is a fast (zippy) woman.

Boys' Names

Ahitub (1 Sam. 22:9)—Means "my brother is goodness" but sounds like taking an elevated bath

Bukki (1 Chron. 6:51)—Your family had better live in Ohio.

Dodo (2 Sam. 23:24)—Father of Elhanan. Even if your child is smart, no one would believe it.

Gog (Ezek. 38:2)—Imagine the headline if he marries Zillah.

Josheb-basshebeth (2 Sam. 23:8)—Gesundheit

Maher-shalal-hash-baz (Isa. 8:3)—Means "speeding is the spoil, hastening is the prey"

Romamti-ezer (1 Chron. 25:4)—Sounds romam-tic except for the "ezer" part

Zaphenath-paneah (Gen. 41:45)—The name Pharaoh gave to Joseph when he married the daughter of a priest. "I, Zaphenath-paneah, take thee, Asenath . . ."

❈ ST. PATRICK'S CATHEDRAL(S) ❈

St. Patrick's Cathedral in New York City is well known, but there are at least twelve St. Patrick's Cathedrals around the world. Three are in Ireland, and ironically only one is Catholic. A church is a cathedral if it is the seat of a bishop; often an existing church has become a cathedral with the founding of a new diocese (area headed by a bishop). Here's a list.

Catholic:

Melbourne, Australia	Armagh, Northern Ireland
Parramatta, Australia	New York, New York
Bridgetown, Barbados	Rochester, New York
Bangalore, India	Thunder Bay, Ontario
Pune (Poona), India	Karachi, Pakistan

Church of Ireland (Anglican):
Armagh, Northern Ireland
Dublin, Ireland

❧ FOUR THEORIES OF ATONEMENT ❧

Jesus saves—but *how?* At the heart of Christian faith is the conviction that the death of Christ made atonement for our sin and reconciled us to God. *Atonement* is another English word for *reconciliation*. Theologians have had different ideas about how this atonement happens.

Theory	Summary of View	Scripture Examples	Major Figures and Venues
Classic or "dramatic"	Atonement is a *work of God*; Christ's death is *God's victory* over the powers of evil, through which people are delivered from them.	2 Corinthians 5:19; Colossians 2:13–15	Church fathers, Eastern Orthodoxy, Martin Luther
Latin or "judicial"	Atonement is the *work of Christ* as representative of mankind; his sacrificial death *pays the price* demanded by God for sin.	Romans 3:24; Old Testament concept of atonement through sacrifice	Anselm of Canterbury, Catholic thought since the Middle Ages, Protestant Orthodoxy after Luther, modern evangelicalism
Moral or "subjective"	Christ's *example* of self-sacrifice creates a *response of love* in people and lifts them to God.	Luke 7:47	Peter Abelard, Friedrich Schleiermacher, Enlightenment and "liberal" movements
Devotional or "pietist"	Through *devotion*, people can enter into Christ's passion and be united with divine love.	Colossians 1:24–25	Thomas à Kempis, mystics, Catholic devotional movements

❧ MEANING OF IHS SYMBOL ❧

This symbol is often found in churches, especially those built with more traditional architecture. It is sometimes said to stand for "In His Service." It originates, however, in the first three letters of the Greek name for Jesus, *Iesous*. It is perhaps more correctly written in Greek small capitals as IHC.

❀ THE WORLD'S ONLY ❀
OFFICIALLY CHRISTIAN NATION

About 4.6 million of Zambia's population of 10 million are Christians. In December 1991, Dr. F. J. T. Chiluba, president of Zambia, declared his nation a Christian state despite the presence of small Muslim and Hindu communities. He saw this declaration as a response to divine intervention in the political transition to the present republic. More important, he believes that the gospel values of love and conscientious living should be the foundation of national life and statecraft. Once a lukewarm Christian, Dr. Chiluba spent time in prison, during which he became immersed in the Scriptures and experienced a reawakening of faith.

❀ RUNNING THE NUMBERS ON KING SOLOMON ❀

- Solomon had 4,000 stalls for his horses (1 Kings 4:26).
- The daily provision for the royal household included 185 bushels of fine flour, 375 bushels of meal, 10 fat oxen, 20 pasture-fed cattle, and 100 sheep and goats (1 Kings 4:22–23).
- He had 12,000 horsemen (1 Kings 4:26).
- He uttered 3,000 proverbs (1 Kings 4:32).
- He composed 1,005 songs (1 Kings 4:32).
- There were 550 chief officers over Solomon's later public works (1 Kings 9:23).
- His seamen brought about 16 tons of gold from Ophir (1 Kings 9:28).
- The queen of Sheba gave Solomon about 4½ tons of gold (1 Kings 10:10).
- Solomon received about 25 tons of gold in a year (1 Kings 10:14).
- He had 1,400 chariots (1 Kings 10:26).
- Solomon could buy chariots from Egypt for about 15 pounds of silver, and horses for about 3¾ pounds, for resale to kings farther north (1 Kings 10:29).
- He had 700 wives (1 Kings 11:3).
- He had 300 concubines (1 Kings 11:3).
- Solomon reigned 40 years over all Israel (1 Kings 11:42).
- Solomon made 200 large shields of beaten gold, each weighing about 7½ pounds, and 300 more shields, each using about 3¾ pounds of gold (1 Kings 10:16–17).

❊ SEVEN RULERS NAMED HEROD ❊

Herod "the Great," a client king within the Roman Empire, had five wives in succession and many children. After his death the Romans divided his kingdom, and his descendants ruled over various parts of it for a century. To make a confusing situation even more so, several of them are sometimes called "Herod II," including one who, apparently, was not a ruler.

Ruler	Territory	Ruled	Comments
Herod the Great	Judea, Samaria, Galilee	39–4 BC	Ruler at the birth of Christ
Herod II Boethius		d. after AD 35	Son of Herod the Great
Herod Archelaus	Judea and Samaria	4 BC– AD 6	Son of Herod the Great; deposed by Rome and banished to Gaul
Herod Antipas	Galilee and Perea	4 BC– AD 39	Son of Herod the Great; executed John the Baptist (Mark 6); later deposed by Rome and banished to Gaul
Herod Philip	"Tetrarchy of Philip"	4 BC– AD 34	Son of Herod the Great; founded Caesarea Philippi
Herod of Chalcis	Chalcis (in Lebanon)	?– AD 48	Grandson of Herod the Great
Herod Agrippa I	Eventually, all former territory of Herod the Great	AD 39–44	Grandson of Herod the Great, brother of Herod of Chalcis
Herod Agrippa II	Chalcis, Tetrarchy of Philip	AD 50–93	Son of Agrippa I; Romans gave him authority to appoint the high priest; Paul made a defense before him (Acts 26)

❧ CHURCH ANNOUNCEMENT "BLOOPERS" ❧

• Miss Charlene Mason sang "I Will Not Pass This Way Again," giving obvious pleasure to the congregation.

• At the evening service tonight, the sermon topic will be "What Is Hell?" Come early and listen to our choir practice.

• The concert held in the Fellowship Hall was a great success. Special thanks are due to the minister's daughter, who labored the whole evening at the piano, which as usual fell on her.

• Eight new choir robes are currently needed, due to the addition of several new members and to the deterioration of some of the older ones.

• The "Over 60 Choir" will be disbanded for the summer with the thanks of the entire church.

• Today's Sermon: "How Much Can a Man Drink?" with hymns from a full choir.

• This being Easter Sunday, we will ask Mrs. Lewis to come forward and lay an egg on the altar.

• For those of you who have children and don't know it, we have a nursery downstairs.

• The church is glad to have with us today as our guest minister the Reverend Green, who has Mrs. Green with him. After the service we request that all remain in the sanctuary for the Hanging of the Greens.

• The sermon this morning: "Jesus Walks on the Water." The sermon tonight: "Searching for Jesus."

• Barbara C. remains in the hospital and needs blood donors for more transfusions. She is also having trouble sleeping and requests tapes of Pastor Jack's sermons.

• During the absence of our pastor we enjoyed the rare privilege of hearing a good sermon when J. F. Scubbs supplied our pulpit.

• The Reverend Merriweather spoke briefly, much to the delight of the audience.

• The pastor will preach his farewell message, after which the choir will sing "Break Forth into Joy."

• The audience is asked to remain seated until the end of the recession.

• This afternoon there will be a meeting in the south and north ends of the church. Children will be baptized at both ends.

• Thursday night—potluck supper. Prayer and medication to follow.

• Remember in prayer the many who are sick of our church and community.

• Due to the Rector's illness, Wednesday's healing services will be discontinued until further notice.

• The peacemaking meeting scheduled for today has been canceled due to a conflict.

• Low Self-Esteem Support Group will meet Thursday at 7 PM. Please use the back door.

• Weight Watchers will meet at 7:00 PM at the First Presbyterian Church. Please use the large double door at the side entrance.

❋ CHURCH ANNOUNCEMENT "BLOOPERS"—CONT. ❋

• The eighth graders will be presenting Shakespeare's *Hamlet* in the church basement on Friday at 7:00 PM. The congregation is invited to attend this tragedy.

• Ladies, don't forget the rummage sale. It is a good chance to get rid of those things not worth keeping around the house. Bring your husbands.

• Next Sunday a special collection will be taken to defray the cost of the new carpet. All those wishing to do something on the new carpet will come forward and do so.

• The outreach committee has enlisted 25 visitors to make calls on people who are not afflicted with any church.

• Irving Benson and Jessie Carter were married on October 24 in the church. So ends a friendship that began in school days.

• Please join us as we show our support for Amy and Alan in preparing for the girth of their first child.

• Don't let worry kill you—let the church help.

• To announce a visit from a missionary: "Come tonight and hear Bertha Belch all the way from Africa."

❋ THE WORLD'S TOP TEN CHRISTIAN NATIONS ❋

This is a list of the world's nations with the largest number of nominal Christians. Of course, in some countries a person might be identified as a Christian only because he or she was baptized in infancy, not because of current participation or practice.

Country	Nominal Christians	Percent of Population
United States	224,457,000	85
Brazil	139,000,000	93
Mexico	86,120,000	99
Russia	80,000,000	60
China	70,000,000	5.7
Germany	67,000,000	83
Philippines	63,470,000	93
United Kingdom	51,060,000	88
Italy	47,690,000	90
France	44,150,000	98

❈ A FEW OF THE 580 PLACES ❈
NAMED AFTER SAINTS IN QUEBEC

At least 580 placenames begin with "Saint" or "Sainte" in Quebec. This does not include many other names incorporating "Saint," "Sainte," or a saint's name, such as Sault St-Louis, Baie St-Paul, or Cap-de-la-Madeleine (St. Mary Magdalene). Here's a short summary:

Distinction	Name	Comments
Longest names	Ste-Catherine-de-la-Jacques-Cartier St-Jacques-le-Majeur-de-Wolfetown	
Shortest names	St-Pie Ste-Foy	French for St. Pius, Pope Pius V From French for "Holy Faith"
Largest City	St-Laurent	Population 74,240
Most Recreational	St-Ferréol-les-Neiges	Near a ski resort; name means "St. Ferreol of the Snows"
Most Obscure	St-Herménégilde	Population 158. Hermengild (died 585) was a prince of the Visigoths in Spain who was imprisoned by his Arian father because of his conversion to the Catholic faith.
Most Laughable	St-Louis-du-Ha! Ha!	Nowhere near the Ha! Ha! River

❈ THREE ENDINGS TO MARK'S GOSPEL ❈

The oldest manuscripts of the Gospel according to Mark end with 16:8, "for they were afraid," but the final word in Greek, *gar*, is one not used to end a sentence. Something is missing. Perhaps the original ending, written on the outside of the rolled-up document, was damaged in transit.

Verses 9–20, printed in most Bibles, come from later manuscripts. There is an alternate ending in other ancient sources, after verse 8: "But they reported briefly to Peter and those with him all that they had been told. And after this, Jesus himself sent out by means of them, from east to west, the sacred and imperishable proclamation of eternal salvation."

One eighth-century manuscript contains both alternate endings after verse 8.

❧ WHAT'S THE DIFFERENCE BETWEEN ❧ A PURITAN AND A PILGRIM?

The Puritans were a Reformed party within the Church of England in the sixteenth to seventeenth centuries. They sought to restructure and renew the church according to biblical principles. They did not leave the established church but considered themselves the purified Church of England. The Separatists, on the other hand, left the established church and formed their own groups in order to worship according to biblical standards. Because England did not tolerate religious diversity, many Separatists lived in Holland.

The settlers of the Plymouth Colony in 1620 were Separatists. In the nineteenth century they began to be called the *Pilgrims*, but originally they were simply the *first-comers*. A larger group of Puritans established the Massachusetts Bay Colony in nearby Salem and Boston in 1630. The two groups differed in their concept of the church but otherwise had a similar theology and worship. Eventually the two colonies were merged into Massachusetts, and people came to think of all of them as Puritans.

As a sidelight, after these two colonies were established, conditions improved in England for those of the Reformed viewpoint, and immigration to New England slowed till after the American Revolution. As a result, the further settlement of New England occurred through expansion of the original group of colonists, leading to a uniform Puritan culture throughout much of the Northeast. New England was the most settled and prosperous part of colonial America, and its culture was influential in shaping that of the developing nation.

❧ HISTORICALLY AFRICAN-AMERICAN ❧ DENOMINATIONS

Several American denominations have a history of serving the African-American community. In some cases they were formed with the assistance and encouragement of their Caucasian counterparts in order to give African-Americans the opportunity to shape their own church life. While they remain predominantly African-American, these groups now welcome Caucasian or other worshipers as well.

African Methodist Episcopal Church • African Methodist Episcopal Zion Church • Christian Methodist Episcopal Church (formerly Colored Methodist Episcopal Church) • Church of God in Christ • National Baptist Convention of America • National Baptist Convention, USA, Inc. • Progressive National Baptist Association

Two groups are more recently formed:
National Missionary Baptist Convention of America
Full Gospel Baptist Church Fellowship

❧ GOOD-LOOKING MEN AND WOMEN OF THE BIBLE ❧

Women
Sarai, wife of Abraham (Gen. 12:11–14)
Rebecca, wife of Isaac (Gen. 24:16)
Rachel, wife of Jacob (Gen. 29:17)
Abigail, wife of Nabal, then David (1 Sam. 25:3)
Bathsheba, wife of Uriah the Hittite, then David (2 Sam. 11:2–3)
Tamar, daughter of David (2 Sam. 13:1)
Tamar, daughter of Absalom (2 Sam. 14:27)
Abishag the Shunamite, nurse for the aged David (1 Kings 1:1–4)
Esther, queen of Persia (Esther 2)
The daughters of Job (Job 42:15)
The king's bride (Ps. 45:10–11)
The bride in the Song of Solomon (Song 4:1, 7)
Judith (apocryphal Book of Judith 8:7)

Men
Joseph, son of Jacob (Gen. 39:6)
Saul, son of Kish (1 Sam. 9:1–2)
David (1 Sam. 16:11–12)
Absalom, son of David (2 Sam. 14:25–26)
An Egyptian warrior slain by Benaiah (2 Sam. 23:21)
Daniel, Hananiah, Mishael, and Azariah (Dan. 1:3–6)
Adonijah, son of David (1 Kings 1:5–6)
The king as a groom (Ps. 45:2)

❧ DEWEY DECIMAL CODES FOR RELIGION ❧

Dewey Decimal Classification
200	Religion (General)
210	Natural religion
220	Bible
230	Christian doctrinal theology
240	Christian moral and devotional
250	Local churches and religious orders
260	Social and ecclesiastical theology
270	History and geography of the church
280	Christian denominations and sects
290	Other religions and comparative religion

❧ MOST REPRINTED HYMNS ❧

More than 5,000 different hymnals have been published in the United States—approximately 1,800 by denominations and 3,200 by independent publishers. Studies of Protestant hymnals from the eighteenth to twentieth centuries have suggested the following are the most popular, not counting Christmas or patriotic songs:

1. "All Hail the Power of Jesus' Name"—Edward Perronet, 1780
2. "Jesus, Lover of My Soul"—Charles Wesley, 1740
3. "Alas! And Did My Savior Bleed?"—Isaac Watts, 1707
4. "How Firm a Foundation"—Rippon's Selection, 1787, based on Isaiah 43:1–5
5. "Am I a Soldier of the Cross?"—Isaac Watts, 1724
6. "Come, Thou Fount of Every Blessing"—Robert Robinson, 1758
7. "Guide Me, O Thou Great Jehovah"—William Williams, 1745
8. "On Jordan's Stormy Banks I Stand"—Samuel Stennett, 1787
9. "Rock of Ages, Cleft for Me"—Augustus M. Toplady, 1776
10. "When I Can Read My Title Clear"—Isaac Watts, 1707

Among Catholic hymnals published more recently, the following hymns are most often reprinted:

1. "Faith of Our Fathers"—Frederick W. Faber, 1849
2. "O God, Our Help in Ages Past"—Isaac Watts, 1719 (Ps. 90)
3. "All Hail the Power of Jesus' Name"—Edward Perronet, 1780
4. "Come, Thou Almighty King"—Anonymous, 1757
5. "Amazing Grace"—John Newton, 1779
6. "Joy to the World"—Isaac Watts, 1719 (Ps. 98)
7. "Holy, Holy, Holy! Lord God Almighty"—Reginald Heber, 1826
8. "From All That Dwell Below the Skies"—Isaac Watts, 1719 (Ps. 117)
9. "Love Divine, All Loves Excelling"—Charles Wesley, 1747
10. "Rejoice, the Lord Is King"—Charles Wesley, 1744

❧ STAINED-GLASS WINDOWS IN ❧
THE NOTRE DAME CATHEDRAL

Many Catholic cathedrals are called *Notre Dame*, but the one in Paris is the best known. It has eighty-two stained-glass windows. Most famous is the circular Rose Window in the south transept, which itself has ninety-one sections. It is said to be the largest stained-glass window in the world, but there are other claimants to this honor, including the Great East Window of the York Minster in England, which is as large as a tennis court.

❀ THE PSALMS BY CHAPTER AND VERSE ❀

Catholic Bibles translated from the Latin Vulgate used a different numbering for the Psalms, based on the Septuagint (ancient Greek Old Testament). Protestant Bibles, and newer Catholic Bibles translated from the Hebrew, use the Hebrew numbering. As a result, the familiar Psalm 23 is Psalm 24 in older Catholic Bibles. The numbering differs by one from Psalm 9 to Psalm 113, and from Psalm 117 to Psalm 146, with additional variations.

Protestant	Catholic
1–8	1–8
9 and 10	9
11–113	10–112
114 and 115	113
116	114 and 115
117–146	116–145
147	146 and 147
148–150	148–150

Additionally, the *verse* numbers in the psalms may differ by one between the English and Hebrew versions. Many of the Psalms begin with a superscription (such as a historical note or directions for performance). In the Hebrew text the superscription is verse 1; in the English version, it is unnumbered.

❀ THE FIRST WOMAN BISHOPS ❀

The concept of *apostolic succession* means that a person is a true bishop only if ordained, or consecrated, by another bishop whose ordination goes back through an unbroken succession of bishops to apostolic times. While other churches and denominations have officers called bishops, only those of the historic Eastern and Western churches and the Anglican churches (a division of the Western church) have bishops in the apostolic succession. Using this criterion, the first known woman bishop was Barbara Clementine Harris, an African-American elected in 1989 as a suffragan (assisting) bishop in the Episcopal Diocese of Massachusetts.

If legend is correct, however, the first female to receive Episcopal ordination was Brigid (St. Bride, died around 523), whom St. Patrick converted to Christianity. She founded the first convent in Ireland at Cill-Dara (Kildare), and Bishop Ibor reportedly consecrated her. The Roman Catholic Church discounts the story.

❦ RESTORATION CHURCHES IN AMERICA ❦

The term *restoration churches* refers to groups that have formed to restore what they believed to be the practice of the New Testament church, renouncing all creeds and holding only to the Bible as their authority. The movement began in North America in the early 1800s and is also called the *Christians-only movement*. It had two main thrusts: (1) emulating the New Testament church, and (2) restoring the unity of the church by avoiding denominational structures.

Over time, the movement divided between these two aims. Those stressing early Christian practices largely withdrew from contact with other churches, while those who sought unity with other churches lost many of their "primitive" or early Christian traits. In the process, the movement to end denominationalism resulted in the formation of many new denominations, though most restorationist groups refuse to be considered denominations and avoid organizations that officially link their local churches.

Because many of these churches call themselves *Christian* or *Churches of Christ*, it is often hard to tell which branch of the movement they belong to.

Groups stemming from the "Christians-only" movement include Christian Church (Disciples of Christ), Christian Churches and Churches of Christ (independent), Churches of Christ (noninstrumental), and International Churches of Christ ("Crossroads" or "Boston" movement).

❦ THE LARGEST CHURCHES IN ❦ THE WORLD AND IN THE UNITED STATES

The world's largest church, in terms of membership, is the Yoido Full Gospel Church of Seoul, Korea, with a reported 780,000 members. The largest known church in Africa is the Deeper Life Bible Church of Lagos, Nigeria, with 85,000 members. Compared to these, the eleven largest congregations in the United States are pikers:

Lakewood Church, Houston, TX—25,000

World Changers, College Park, GA—23,100

New Birth Church, Atlanta, GA—23,000

Calvary Chapel of Costa Mesa, Santa Ana, CA—20,000

The Potter's House, Dallas, TX—18,500

Second Baptist Church, Houston, TX—18,000

Southeast Christian Church, Louisville, KY—17,900

First Assembly of God, Phoenix, AZ—17,500

Willow Creek Community Church, South Barrington, IL—17,100

Calvary Chapel of Fort Lauderdale, Fort Lauderdale, FL—17,000

Saddleback Valley Community Church, Lake Forest, CA—15,000

❧ FAMOUS AFRICANS OF CHURCH HISTORY ❧

These are Christian leaders who lived in or came from Africa. Those listed from North or South Africa are not black; Ethiopians also are racially different from black Africans.

Tertullian (160–220), Carthage (in modern Tunisia), first Christian theologian to write in Latin

Commodian (third century), Christian Latin poet of North Africa

Cyprian (died 258), bishop of Carthage and writer of treatises

Ezana, king of Ethiopia (ruled 325–360), converted by the missionary Frumentius (died 380), made Ethiopia one of the world's first Christian nations

Athanasius (296–373), bishop of Alexandria, Egypt; leading opponent of the Arian movement

Donatus (fourth century), leader of a strict Christian sect eventually declared schismatic

Augustine (354–430), bishop of Hippo (in modern Tunisia), influential theologian and Doctor of the Church

Cyril (died 444), patriarch of Alexandria, considered a Doctor of the Church

John Ezzidio (1810–1872), Sierra Leone, former slave, Wesleyan Methodist minister and prominent businessman

Samuel Ajayi Crowther (1806–1891), Yoruba (Nigeria), first African Anglican bishop, 1864

Edward Wilmot Blyden (1832–1912), Liberia, Presbyterian minister and leading African intellectual of the nineteenth century

Andrew Murray (1828–1917), South Africa, Dutch Reformed minister and influential writer in spiritual formation

Haile Selassie (1892–1975), emperor of Ethiopia, styled "King of Kings and Lion of Judah." As emperor he was head of the Ethiopian Church and an opponent of international aggression. His name, which he took at his enthronement, means "Force of Trinity."

David DuPlessis (1905–1987), South African Pentecostal active in the ecumenical movement

Festo Kivengere (1919–1988), Anglican bishop of Kigezi, Uganda, who withstood the dictator Idi Amin

Ndabaningi Sithole (1922–2000), Zimbabwe, Congregational minister and politician

Abel Muzorewa (born 1925), Zimbabwe (Rhodesia), Methodist bishop and first prime minister of Zimbabwe, 1979

❧ THE MAYFLOWER COMPACT ❧

The settlers of Plymouth reached the shores of America in 1620. Before landing, their leaders drew up an agreement that everyone aboard had to sign. It's known as the Mayflower Compact, and it established the basis for a stable government in the new colony, dedicated to the advancement of the Christian faith. This is the original wording of the compact, from William Bradford's handwriting, in which the word *the* is written y^e. All free adult males, and some of the servants, signed the document.

In ye name of God, Amen. We whose names are underwriten, the loyall subjects of our dread soveraigne Lord King James by ye grace of God, of Great Britaine, Franc, & Ireland king, defender of ye faith, &c.

Haveing undertaken, for ye glorie of God, and advancemente of ye Christian faith, and honour of our king & countrie, a voyage to plant ye first colonie in ye Northerne parts of Virginia, doe by these presents solemnly & mutualy in ye presence of God, and one of another, covenant & combine our selves togeather into a civill body politick; for our better ordering & preservation & furtherance of ye ends aforesaid; and by vertue hearof, to enacte, constitute, and frame such just & equall lawes, ordinances, acts, constitutions, & offices, from time to time, as shall be thought most meete & convenient for ye generall good of ye Colonie: unto which we promise all due submission and obedience. In witnes wherof we have hereunder subscribed our names at Cap-Codd ye 11 of November, in ye year of the raigne of our soveraigne lord, King James of England, France, & Ireland ye eighteenth, and of Scotland ye fiftie fourth. An^O: Dom. 1620.

❧ FAVORITE BIBLE VERSIONS IN THE UNITED STATES ❧

A widely reported survey revealed that 34 percent of Protestant pastors in the United States currently favor the New International Version (NIV) Bible. Twenty-four percent say The King James Version (KJV) is their favorite. Pastors ranked the New Revised Standard Version (NRSV) as third, with 17 percent. Ten percent prefer The New King James Version (NKJV), while another 9 percent of pastors use the New American Standard Bible (NASB). More than 2 percent of the 500 pastors surveyed preferred no particular version. (The other 4 percent covers all the versions other than those named, in percentages too small to mention.) Pastors of evangelical or conservative churches prefer the NIV and KJV, with Pentecostal and charismatic pastors heavily favoring the King James. Pastors of mainline or "liberal" churches, on the other hand, prefer the NRSV by a wide margin.

❀ DOCTORS OF THE CHURCH ❀

More than thirty figures from Christian history have been regarded as "doctors of the church" because of their holy lives and the benefit the church has derived from their teaching.

The ancient church of the West recognized four doctors:	The Eastern Church recognized three doctors:
1. St. Gregory the Great	1. St. John Chrysostom
2. St. Ambrose	2. St. Basil
3. St. Augustine	3. St. Gregory Nazianzen
4. St. Jerome	

St. Thomas Aquinas was added to the list in the sixteenth century, and since then popes have added others, including:

St. Anselm • St. Peter Damian • St. Francis de Sales • St. John of the Cross • St. Teresa of Avila • Most recently named is St. Thérèse of Lisieux, in 1997.

The doctors are often known by distinctive epithets. St. Thomas Aquinas is known as *Doctor angelicus*, the "angelic Doctor"; William of Ockham is known as *Doctor invincibilis*; and St. Albertus Magnus as *Doctor universalis*, *Doctor venerabilis*, or *Doctor expertus*.

❀ THE LARGEST U.S. DENOMINATIONS ❀

Roman Catholic	50,873,000
Baptist	33,830,000
Methodist/Wesleyan	14,140,000
Lutheran	9,580,000
Presbyterian	5,595,000
Pentecostal/Charismatic	4,407,000
Episcopal/Anglican	3,451,000
Mormon	2,787,000
Churches of Christ	2,503,000
Nondenominational	2,489,000
Congregational/United Church of Christ	1,378,000
Jehovah's Witnesses	1,331,000

❀ CHILDREN OF THE POPES ❀

The Catholic Church traces the origin of the papacy to the apostle Peter, who was married (Jesus healed his mother-in-law, Matt. 8:14–15). Before 1139, when celibacy was made a requirement for Latin Rite clergy, at least four popes and many bishops, priests, and deacons were married. Pope Adrian II (reigned 862–872) was a married layman; a relative of the rival pope Anastasius murdered his wife and daughter. After 1139 Pope Clement IV (1265–1268) was a widower and the antipope Felix V was a married layman. Other clergy married after 1139 despite church policy.

A few popes were sons of popes. Innocent I (reigned 401–417) was the son of Anastasius I, Silverus (536–537) was the son of Hormidas, and John XI (931–935) was the son of Sergius III. Ten other popes were sons of clergymen. Many clergy had children through unmarried alliances both before and after 1139, and at least five popes fathered children after the celibacy rule was issued.

The most famous child of a pope is Lucrezia Borgia, daughter of Pope Alexander VI (Rodrigo Borgia, reigned 1492–1503). Lucrezia was heavily involved in family turmoil and intrigue, though perhaps not as the instigator of it, as she has often been portrayed. Pope Alexander VI had four children by Lucrezia's mother, Vanozza Catanei, and later had a mistress, Giulia Farnese, whom local wags dubbed the "bride of Christ."

❀ THE FIVE POINTS OF CALVINISM ❀

Here are the well-known "five points of Calvinism" and a brief explanation of each.

Total Depravity	People are unable to deliver themselves from bondage to sin.
Unconditional Election	People can do nothing to merit God's choice of them.
Limited Atonement	Christ's death atones for the sin of those whom God has chosen.
Irresistible Grace	Those to whom God has given life find his grace in Christ irresistible.
Perseverance of the Saints	Since salvation is God's gift, the Christian cannot fall away from it.

❧ CHRISTIAN POETS ❧

Edmund Spenser (1552–1599) . . . . English Renaissance poet famous for *The Faerie Queene*, an allegory of the struggle between good and evil

John Donne (1572–1631) . . . . Considered the greatest of the English "metaphysical poets," whose works are marked by an intense and sustained spiritual fervor

George Herbert (1593–1633). . . . . One of the metaphysical poets

John Milton (1608–1674) . . . . English Puritan writer, author of the best-seller *Paradise Lost* and considered one of the greatest poets of the English language

Henry Vaughan (1622–1695). . . . . One of the metaphysical poets

William Cowper (1731–1800) . . . . English poet and hymn writer

William Blake (1757–1827) . . . . Unconventional and obscure English poet and artist, but his work had a great influence on later Romanticism

Emily Dickinson (1830–1886) . . . . Rarely left her home in Amherst, Massachusetts, but came to be considered one of the greatest original poets in American literature

Anna Shipton (died 1901). . . . . English devotional poet of the late 1800s; though little remembered today, she was a favorite of C. H. Spurgeon and D. L. Moody

George MacDonald (1824–1905). . . . . . Scottish writer influential for C. S. Lewis; much of his fiction has recently been republished in updated versions

Amy Carmichael (1867–1951) . . . . Missionary in India and a prolific writer of devotional books and poetry

Dorothy L. Sayers (1893–1957) . . . . . . Anglican writer recognized for the doctrinal depth of her poetry and other works

Wystan Hugh Auden (1907–1973). . . . . English poet of probing depth, who adopted a Christian perspective later in life but had gender issues

❧ CHRISTIAN POETS—CONT. ❧

Helen Steiner Rice (1900–1981) . . . . Believed to have written several million poems, including greeting-card verse and ten volumes; donated her royalties to her Methodist church in Cincinnati

Vassar Miller (1924–1998) . . . . Considered by some to be the Emily Dickinson of the twentieth century

Madeleine L'Engle (born 1918) . . . . Has written poetry in addition to her popular Christian fiction

❧ PASSAGES OF SCRIPTURE ❧ REPEATED IN SCRIPTURE

Not counting quotations from the Old Testament in the New, many portions of Scripture repeat material found elsewhere. This is a partial list. It is not always certain which of the doubled portions is the "original." Some repeats contain slight alterations.

- Exodus 20:1–17 (the Ten Commandments) is repeated in Deuteronomy 5:6–21.
- Numbers 7:13–17, the list of gifts of the leader of the tribe of Judah, is repeated verbatim eleven times (vv. 18–83) for the gifts of the other eleven tribal leaders.
- Joshua 24:29–32 is repeated in Judges 2:6–9.
- 2 Kings 18:13–20:19 is repeated in Isaiah 36:1–38:11 and 38:21–39:8.
- 2 Chronicles 36:22–23 is repeated in Ezra 1:1–3.
- Psalm 14 is repeated almost verbatim as Psalm 53, with "the LORD" changed to "God."
- Psalm 15:1–4 is repeated in Psalm 24:3–4.
- Psalm 108 is a repeat of Psalms 57:7–11 and 60:5–12.
- Psalm 135 is made up entirely of phrases from other psalms.
- Isaiah 2:2–4 is repeated in Micah 4:1–3. (Joel 3:10 reverses the thought of the last verse.)
- Large portions of the Gospel of Mark are repeated in the Gospels of Matthew and Luke.
- Ephesians 5:18–6:9 is repeated as Colossians 3:16–25.

❀ LITERARY GENRES FOUND IN SCRIPTURE ❀

A literary *genre* is a type of literature, such as a novel, a poem, or a technical manual. These are some of the genres found in the Holy Scriptures, with examples. There are other ways of organizing the classifications, and often the literary forms are mixed. The categories assigned to biblical material do not always reflect the form; for example, the Letter of James is more a sermon than a letter, and the Revelation to John is more a drama than a prophecy.

Poetry Genres

Prophetic Oracle ..... Utterances of "the word of the LORD," throughout the Prophets and in some of the Psalms (e.g., 82, 91)

Hymn .... Many of the Psalms, such as 8, 46, 100, 150, and early Christian hymns in Luke 1–2 or the Revelation to John

Lament .... The majority of Psalms; also found in the Prophets and in Lamentations

Wedding Poetry ...... Psalm 45, the Song of Solomon

Narrative Genres

Story .... A narrative of unfolding events, historical or biographical. This is a major genre found in most parts of the Bible, such as Genesis–Numbers, Joshua–Chronicles, parts of the prophetic books, and the Acts of the Apostles. There are subcategories.

Gospel .... Not a standard history-biography but a specialized proclamation of Jesus as Messiah

Parable .... An illustrative story, developed most fully by Jesus in Matthew–Luke but found elsewhere

Instructional/Wisdom Genres

Law .... Biblical law is more instructional than legal, especially the conditional ("casuistic") law of Exodus

Proverb .... Short instructional sayings, as in the book of Proverbs

Reflection .... Ecclesiastes

Sermon .... Preaching based on law or Christian principles, such as Deuteronomy or the book of James

Epistle Genres

Circular letter .... The letters of Paul to various churches, or the letters of Revelation 1–3

Official letter .... Letters to and from officials in the Persian Empire, in the book of Ezra

✸ LITERARY GENRES FOUND IN SCRIPTURE—CONT. ✸

Dramatic Genres
Apocalypse . . . . Daniel and the Revelation to John
Dialogue . . . . The book of Job

Liturgical Genres
Liturgical directives . . . Instructions for performing sacrifices, etc., as in Leviticus
Laws for recitation . . . The Ten Commandments and other groupings ("apodic-tic" or absolute law)
Festival liturgies . . . . . . Psalms 50, 118

Genealogy
Ancestor or . . . . 1 Chronicles or the genealogies of Jesus in Matthew and
family lists   Luke

✸ HOW A POPE IS ELECTED ✸

The pope, or Holy Father, is the bishop of Rome and is elected by the clergy of his diocese. Because he oversees the Roman Catholic Church worldwide, the priests of the Diocese of Rome (known as the College of Cardinals) are drawn from all across the Catholic Church, most being bishops or archbishops. They are nominally the pastors of churches of the Diocese of Rome, but they normally spend their time administering their own regions or other departments of the church (called *Congregations* or *Dicasteries*).

Pope John Paul II revised the rules for electing a pope. Cardinals must be under eighty years old to take part in the election, and the number of those entitled to vote is limited to 120. When a pope dies, this "conclave" of cardinals spends two to three weeks mourning, then gathers in the Vatican's Sistine Chapel. The electors write the name of their choice on a secret ballot; they are sworn to secrecy about the deliberations and must have no contact with the outside world during the process.

Designated officials tally the ballots. A candidate must receive two-thirds of the eligible votes, but after thirty unsuccessful attempts, a simple majority will elect the new pope. The ballots are burned after each vote as a signal to the outside world, with a substance to turn the smoke white if a new pope has been elected. The new pope chooses the name he will use, and the dean of the College of Cardinals introduces him from the Vatican's main balcony with the words *Habemus Papam*, "We have a pope." An inauguration ceremony follows.

In theory, even a layman can be elected to the papacy, but the last time this happened was in 1059. Since 1378, all popes have been chosen from the College of Cardinals.

❋ THE AMAZING SANTA ❋

Santa Claus, in whatever local disguise is appropriate, is responsible for delivering gifts to good children on the night before Christmas. There are approximately two billion children in the world, but Santa does not handle Muslim, Buddhist, Hindu, Jewish, or Jehovah's Witnesses children or those from other groups that do not celebrate Christmas, leaving him with a clientele of around 378 million.

There is an average of 3.5 children per family, making 108 million homes for him to visit (assuming at least 1 good child in each). Given the rotation of the earth and different time zones, he has 31 hours to work with, making 822.6 visits per second, during each of which he has to pick the correct gifts, descend the chimney, distribute the gifts and fill stockings, eat whatever refreshments have been set out for him, and return to his sleigh. Assuming children are evenly distributed around the earth's landmass, he must travel approximately 75.5 million miles, while working in rest stops and time to change into the appropriate costume for the area visited.

Santa's sleigh must carry approximately a 2-pound gift for each child, of whatever type is the current favorite for boys and girls in the visited regions. Assuming an 85 percent ratio of good children to the total, Santa's sleigh must carry a payload of 321,300 tons, not counting the weight of the massive sleigh nor of Santa himself, who is known to have an obesity challenge (conservative estimates place his weight at 250 pounds).

A standard reindeer can pull about half a ton; assuming that flying reindeer can pull 10 times that amount, 64,620 reindeer are required. The average male reindeer weighs 203 pounds at this time of year, increasing the total weight of cargo and propulsion engine to 327,822 tons. When in motion between visits, Santa and his vehicle are traveling at about 650 miles per second, or 3,000 times the speed of sound. This mass traveling at such a velocity would normally heat up through atmospheric resistance to the point of near-instantaneous vaporization. Moreover, Santa is subjected to centrifugal forces 17,500 times that of gravity, being pinned to the back of his sleigh by around 4,315,000 pounds of force.

It's a miracle that even good children receive any Christmas gifts at all.

❋ THE FIVE POINTS OF ARMINIANISM ❋

These are the "five points of Arminianism."

Destiny for salvation is conditional on our response to God.
All people are offered salvation in the atonement of Christ.
It takes the work of the Spirit to create faith in us.
Saving grace is necessary, but we can resist it.
Yes, it is possible to fall away from God's grace.

❊ WELL-KNOWN WOMEN OF CHRISTIAN HISTORY ❊

Susanna Wesley

Helena (247–327) . . Mother of Emperor Constantine, identified many sites in the Holy Land associated with the life of Christ

Monica (331–387) . . Mother of Augustine, influential in his conversion to Christianity

Héloïse (1095–1164) Mistress and secret wife of Peter Abelard, became head of an abbey of nuns

Hildegard von . . . . . German mystic and
Bingen (1098–1179) influential writer, head of a convent

Julian (Juliana) of . . . . English mystic who lived in solitude but was influential
Norwich (1342–1413) through her writing

Joan of Arc (1412–1431) . . Visionary and martyr, patron saint of France

Catherine of Aragon . . . . Henry VIII's annulment of their marriage led to the
(1485–1536) Church of England's break with Rome

Teresa of Avila . . . . Reformed the Carmelite order, a mystic and authority
(1515–1582) on prayer

Elizabeth I (1533–1603) Developed England into the strongest Protestant nation of the time

Susanna Wesley . . . . Mother of John and Charles, influential in their spiritual
(1669–1742) formation

Catherine Winkworth . . . Translator of many well-known hymns from German
(1829–1878) to English

Catherine Booth . . . . Cofounder of the Salvation Army
(1829–1890)

Thérèse of Lisieux . . . . . . French nun and devotional writer, canonized in 1925
(1873–1897)

Fanny Crosby Van . . . . . . Blind poetess of New York City, published more than two
Alstyne (1823–1915) thousand hymns, many of which are still in use

Aimee Semple . . . . Evangelist, founder of the Foursquare Gospel Church
McPherson (1890–1944)

❀ HISTORIC ORDERS OF THE CATHOLIC CHURCH ❀

In Roman Catholic terminology, the words *religious* and *secular* have special meanings. The *secular* clergy are those assigned to the local churches or parishes, while the *religious* are members of religious orders (monks, nuns, and priests). The religious orders own and operate many of the institutions of the Catholic Church, which in 1992 were said to number 6,200 hospitals or sanitariums; 27,000 homes for the elderly, homeless, or handicapped; 80,600 elementary or primary schools; and 6,400 colleges and universities. The largest orders are the Franciscans, with more than 100,000 members in both men's and women's branches; the Jesuits, with 23,000; and the Salesians, with 17,000.

Common Name	Principal Full Name	Initials	Gender	Founder, Year	Emphases
Augustinians*	Order of St. Augustine	O.S.A.	M, F	Eleventh century	Higher education
Benedictines	Order of St. Benedict	O.S.B.	M, F	Unknown, sixth century	Community life
Carmelites	Order of Our Lady of Mt. Carmel	O.Carm.	M, F	Unknown, around 1150	Many areas of service, including missions
Discalced Carmelites	Order of Discalced Carmelites	O.C.D.	M, F	Teresa of Avila, 1568	Contemplative life
Divine Word Missionaries	Society of the Divine Word	S.V.D.	M	Arnold Janssens, 1875	Missions
Dominicans	Order of Friars Preachers *and many other groups*	O.P.	M, F	Dominic de Guzman, 1205	Doctrine, education
Franciscans	Order of Friars Minor *and many other groups*	O.F.M.	M, F	Francis of Assisi, 1209	Functions include schools, missions, and custody of Holy Land sites
Jesuits	Society of Jesus	S.J.	M	Ignatius Loyola 1540	Higher education

❧ HISTORIC ORDERS OF THE ❧ CATHOLIC CHURCH—CONT.

Common Name	Principal Full Name	Initials	Gender	Founder, Year	Emphases
Lasallians	Brothers of the Christian	F.S.C.	M	Jean-Baptiste de La Salle, 1680	Schools
Marists	Society of Mary	S.M.	M, F	1816	Many areas of service
Missionaries of Charity	Missionaries of Charity	M.C.	M, F	Mother Teresa, 1948	Homes for sick and dying
Paulists	Paulist Fathers	C.S.P.	M	Isaac Hecker, 1858	Education, publishing
Redemptorists	Congregation of the Most Holy Redeemer	C.SS.R.	M	Alphonsus Liguori, 1732	Missions
Salesians	Salesians of Don Bosco			Don Bosco, 1859	Schools
Salvatorians	Society of the Divine Savior	S.D.S.	M, F	Francis Jordan, 1881	Missions
Sisters of Charity**	Sisters of Charity		F	Elizabeth Ann Seton, 1810	Work with the poor
Servites	Order of Friar Servants of Mary	O.S.M.	M	Group, 1240	Many areas of service
Sisters, Servants of Mary	Sisters, Servants of Mary	S.M.	F	Maria Soledad, 1851	Nursing homes
Viatorians	Clerics of Saint Viator	O.S.V.	M	Louis Querbes, 1831	Schools

*The most famous Augustinian is Martin Luther.
**Many groups are called Sisters (or Brothers) of Charity, going back to St. Vincent de Paul, 1633.

❊ THE FOUR HORSEMEN OF THE APOCALYPSE ❊

In chapter 6 of the Revelation to John (called the *Apocalypse*), the Lamb is given a scroll of seven seals, containing the judgments to come upon the land. As each of the first four seals is opened, John sees a horse and rider come forth. The four horsemen are

The Four Horsemen of the Apocalypse

1. A rider on a white horse, with a bow, who is given a crown and rides forth to conquer

2. A rider on a red horse, given a great sword and sent forth to cause people to kill one another

3. A rider on a black horse, holding a balance; a voice describes the impending high cost of food, but with the admonition, "do not harm the oil and wine"

4. Death, riding a pale horse, followed by Hades, given power to kill a fourth of the land's population by sword, famine, pestilence, or wild animals

Some view the "four horsemen" as a picture of judgments yet to occur, others see them as symbolic of ongoing conditions resulting from human sinfulness, and some see in the four horsemen a description of conditions in Judea during the time of the Jewish revolt against Rome and the destruction of Jerusalem and its temple in AD 70.

❊ PRESBYTERIAN BODIES IN NORTH AMERICA ❊

Associate Reformed Presbyterian Church • Bible Presbyterian Church • Cumberland Presbyterian Church • Evangelical Presbyterian Church • Free Presbyterian Church • Korean American Presbyterian Church • Orthodox Presbyterian Church • Presbyterian Church in America • Presbyterian Church (USA) • Reformed Presbyterian Church of North America • Reformed Presbyterian Church (Covenanted) • Second Cumberland Presbyterian Church in the United States

❃ DENOMINATIONS THAT ORDAIN ❃ WOMEN AS PASTORS OR PRIESTS

Paul, in Galatians 3:28, wrote that "there is neither Jew nor Greek, there is neither slave nor free, there is neither male nor female; for you are all one in Christ Jesus." Some Christian groups take this to mean that women may be admitted to the ranks of the ordained ministry. Others, such as the Unitarian Universalist Association, take their cue more from the feminist movement than from Scripture. Churches that ordain women include

American Baptist Churches in the USA ● Assemblies of God ● Christian Reformed Church ● Church of England and other national Anglican bodies (some bishops do not) ● Disciples of Christ ● Episcopal Church, USA (some dioceses do not) ● "Evangelical Church" (Lutheran) of Germany, Denmark, and other European countries ● Evangelical Covenant Church ● Evangelical Lutheran Church of America ● Holiness groups including the Church of God (Anderson, Indiana) and the Church of the Nazarene ● Mennonites ● National Association of Congregational Christian Churches ● Presbyterian Church (USA) ● Salvation Army ● Society of Friends (Quakers) ● Unitarian Universalist Association ● United Church of Canada ● United Church of Christ ● United Church of Christ in the Philippines (merger of many Protestant bodies) ● United Methodist Church

❃ A TYPICAL "SINNER'S PRAYER" ❃

Those making their first commitment as Christians often say the Sinner's Prayer. The prayer has many variations, but they all have the same structure:

1. Acknowledging sin against God
2. Appealing for his forgiveness
3. Affirming belief in Jesus' death and resurrection on one's behalf
4. Asking Jesus to take control of one's life and change it
5. Accepting responsibility for living according to God's will

Based on the above, this could be a typical sinner's prayer:

I need you, Lord Jesus, because I know I have disobeyed God and become separated from him. Forgive my sin and cleanse me. Thank you that you died and rose again to give me new life. Take control of my life and help me live as the person you want me to be. I promise to be God's servant, with the help of his Holy Spirit. Amen.

❦ TWO CHERUBIM OR FOUR? ❦

The ark of the covenant was the symbol of Yahweh's presence with Israel. The *cherubim* were winged figures of hammered gold on the cover of the ark (Exod. 25:18–22). In addition, two cherubim about eighteen feet tall were placed in the inner sanctuary (holy of holies) of the temple of Solomon, where their wings overspread the ark (1 Kings 6:23–28). Thus there were *four* cherubim associated with the presence of the Lord, not counting those carved on the doors of the temple.

The cherubim were not "cherubs" as we know them—the chubby winged children of Michelangelo's painting. They were probably more like the awesome composite guardian figures that have been excavated in the palaces of ancient Assyrian rulers—winged figures with body features of the ox and the lion and the head of a man. They were the symbolic guardians of a royal throne and fulfilled this role in Israel as well: "Thou who art enthroned upon the cherubim, shine forth" (Ps. 80:1).

The prophet Ezekiel was a priest (Ezek. 1:3) and would have had access to the temple's inner sanctuary. The description of the four living creatures in his vision of the Lord's glory (Ezek. 1:5–11) is patterned after the appearance of the cherubim, and the four living creatures of the apostle John's vision (Rev. 4:7) are similar. These four cherubim-like figures became the traditional Christian symbols of the four evangelists or gospel writers: Matthew (winged man), Mark (winged lion), Luke (winged ox), and John (eagle).

❦ LEAST RELIGIOUS STATES IN THE UNITED STATES ❦

Hawaii, Oregon, and Washington are the least religious states in the United States. A 2000 survey indicated that as many as 52 percent of Hawaiians identify with no religion; of the remainder, 29 percent are Christian and the others are divided among non-Christian religions. (Hawaii has a large ethnic Japanese population.) Seventeen percent of Oregonians report themselves to be unaffiliated with any religion. In Washington the figure is 14 percent. One report says the percentage of nonreligious in the U.S. is 7 percent. However, the 2000 survey claimed that 14.1 percent of Americans are "secular," with 76.5 claiming to be Christian. The remaining 9.4 percent are reported to be adherents of non-Christian religions or of unknown preference.

❄ NOTABLE CHURCH ARCHITECTS ❄

Architect	Lived	Style	Example
Abbot Suger	1081–1155	Gothic architecture (pioneer)	Abbey of St-Denis, France
Giacomo della Porta	1532–1604	Classical-Baroque	St. Peter's Basilica, Rome
Christopher Wren	1632–1723	English Baroque	St. Paul's Cathedral and many churches in London
Charles Bullfinch	1763–1844	American classical	St. Stephen's Church, Boston (originally New North Congregational Society)
Henry Hobson Richardson	1838–1886	Romanesque revival	Trinity Church, Boston
William Butterfield	1814–1900	Victorian Gothic	All Saints Church, Margaret Street, London
John Francis Bentley	1839–1902	Victorian Byzantine	Westminster Cathedral (Catholic), London
George Frederick Bodley	1827–1907	Medieval styles	National Cathedral, Washington, D.C
Bertram Grosvenor Goodhue	1869–1924	Modern Gothic, Romanesque	St. Patrick's Cathedral, New York
Antonio Gaudi	1852–1926	Expressionist	La Sagrada Familia, Barcelona
Eliel Saarinen	1873–1950	Art Nouveau or "Modern"	First Christian Church, Columbus, Indiana
Eero Saarinen	1910–1961	"International"	North Christian Church, Columbus, Indiana

❄ THREE CHRISTMAS ISLANDS ❄

The famous Christmas Island of Micronesia in the South Pacific is part of the Republic of Kiribati. Captain James Cook discovered it on December 24, 1777. Another Christmas Island, part of Australia, is in the Indian Ocean. Captain William Mynors discovered it on December 25, 1643. Nova Scotia's Christmas Island is not an island but a village. There are two stories of how it got its name: (1) an Indian chief called Christmas is buried on the small offshore island, (2) a team of surveyors named it after finishing their work on Christmas Day.

❊ THE COLLECT, A PATTERN FOR PRAYER ❊

The *collect* is a short prayer that Anglican, Lutheran, and other liturgical churches use in worship. It is called a *collect* because it "collects" the thoughts of the worshipers into one statement at appropriate points in the service. But collects aren't just random prayers; they have a specific structure. Here is one way a collect could be structured:

1. Address to God
2. Descriptive clause about God, i.e., what it is about God that encourages the purpose of the collect
3. Petition or thanksgiving
4. Reason for, or desired outcome of, prayer
5. Ending

Example:
(1) Almighty God, (2) unto whom all hearts are open, all desires known, and from whom no secrets are hid: (3) Cleanse the thoughts of our hearts by the inspiration of thy Holy Spirit, (4) that we may perfectly love thee and worthily magnify thy holy Name; (5) through Christ our Lord. Amen.

❊ BIRTH ORDERS OF SOME CHRISTIAN LEADERS ❊

Brother Andrew (Andy Van Der Bijl) .... Fourth of six
Dietrich Bonhoeffer .... Sixth of eight (had a twin sister)
William Carey .... Oldest of four
Amy Carmichael .... Oldest of seven
Billy Graham .... Oldest of four
Pope John Paul II (Karol Wojtyla) .... Youngest of three (one died in infancy)
C. S. Lewis (Clive Staples Lewis) .... Younger of two
David Livingston .... Second of seven
Oral Roberts .... Youngest of five
Marion G. "Pat" Robertson .... Younger of two
Alexander Solzhenitsyn .... Only child
Billy Sunday (William Ashley Sunday) .... Younger of two
Corrie ten Boom .... Youngest of five
Mother Teresa (Agnes Gonxha Bojaxhiu) .... Youngest of four
John Wesley .... Fifteenth of nineteen
Charles Wesley .... Eighteenth of nineteen
Susanna Wesley (mother of John and Charles) ...... Twenty-fifth of twenty-five

❈ SUPPOSED SAYINGS OF JESUS ❈
NOT FOUND IN SCRIPTURE

Sayings of Jesus exist outside the four Gospels. Paul quoted such a saying in Acts 20:35, "It is more blessed to give than to receive." Jesus also spoke in the Revelation to John. Some editions of the Bible print all the words of Christ in red, highlighting these sayings.

There are, however, other sayings that have come down to us outside the Bible itself, in the writings of the church fathers or in ancient manuscripts. Scholars call these sayings the *agrapha*. Biblical scholars share no universal agreement as to the authenticity of any of them, but a number of prominent scholars consider the following to have the ring of a genuine saying of Jesus.

- Jesus saw a man working on the Sabbath and said to him, "Man, if you know what you are doing you are blessed. But if you don't know, you are cursed and a transgressor against the law."—Codex Bezae (D), in place of Luke 6:5

- "He who is near me is near the fire; he who is far from me is far from the kingdom."—Quoted by Origen

- "No man can obtain the kingdom of heaven, who has not passed through temptation."—Quoted by Tertullian, in the passion narrative before the Garden of Gethsemane

- "I choose for myself the best; the best are those whom my Father in heaven has given me."—Quoted by Eusebius, citing the lost Gospel of the Hebrews

- "Those who are with me have not understood me."—Quoted in the apocryphal Acts of Peter

- "And never be joyful, except when you look upon your brother in love."—Quoted by Jerome, in commenting on Ephesians 5:3–4

- "And pray for your enemies. For he who is not against you is for you, and he who stands far off today will be near you tomorrow."—Oxyrhynchus Papyrus 1224

- "Be approved moneychangers who reject much, but keep the good."—Quoted by Clement of Alexandria in *Stromata*

- "Lift up the stone, and there you will find me; split the wood, and I am there."—Oxyrhynchus Papyrus 1

- "Where one is alone, there I am there also; and where two are, there I am also."—Quoted by Ephraem Syrus

- "Jesus, on whom be peace, has said, 'This world is a bridge. Pass over it, but do not build your dwelling there.'"—On the wall of the ruin of a mosque near Delhi, India, built by Akbar the Great Mogul (1542–1605)

❧ FAMOUS EXCOMMUNICATES ❧

Early Christian leaders deemed heretics were excommunicated (removed from the church). These are some well-known or powerful people who have been excommunicated since the year 1000:

Pope Leo IX and Michael I Cerularius, patriarch of Constantinople—Excommunicated each other in 1054, the official break between the Eastern and Western churches

Henry IV, Holy Roman Emperor—Excommunicated in 1076 for refusing to recognize the authority of Pope Gregory VII and declaring him deposed

Henry VIII of England—Excommunicated in 1533 by Pope Clement VII for annulment of his marriage to Catherine of Aragon and remarriage to Anne Boleyn

Martin Luther, Reformer—Excommunicated in 1521 by Pope Leo X

Elizabeth I of England—Excommunicated in 1570 by Pope Pius V for heresy in claiming to head the Church in England

Giordano (Filippo) Bruno, astronomer—Excommunicated in 1589 by the Lutheran Church of Helmstedt, burned by the Catholic Inquisition in 1593

José María Morelso, priest—Excommunicated around 1813 for leading a Mexican revolt against Spain. He was executed in 1815; a Mexican state is named after him.

Lev Tolstoi, writer—Excommunicated in 1901 by the Russian Holy Synod for departure from Orthodox teaching (We know him as Leo Tolstoy.)

Father Leonard Feeney—Excommunicated in 1953 by Pope Pius XII for refusing to submit to ecclesiastical authority and tone down his harsh, exclusivist teaching

Nikos Kazantzakis, writer—Excommunicated in 1954 by the Greek Orthodox Church for writing the novel *The Last Temptation of Christ*

Juan Perón, Argentine dictator—Excommunicated in 1955 for legalizing divorce and prostitution

Archbishop Marcel Lefebvre—Excommunicated in 1988 by Cardinal Bernardin Gantin for an irregular consecration of bishops and opposition to Vatican II changes

A Theological Miscellany

❀ CHRISTIAN HUMANITARIANS ❀

A humanitarian is a person who promotes human welfare and social reform. Christian faith has motivated many humanitarians of the Western world. These are a few of them.

William Wilberforce (1759–1833) . . . . . British Member of Parliament who secured the abolition of slavery and promoted missions and the Bible Society

George Mueller (1805–1898) . . . . Founder of children's homes in England and leader of the Brethren movement

William (1821–1912) and . . . . Evangelists with an outreach to the poor
Catherine (1829–1890) Booth of England; they founded the Salvation Army

Florence Nightingale (1820–1910) . . . . . English pioneer of nursing and modern hospitals; she described her nurses as "handmaidens of the Lord"

Clara Barton (1821–1912) . . . . Organizer of the American Red Cross. She was a Universalist, which was originally not a Unitarian movement.

Dorothy Day (1897–1980) . . . . Convert to Catholicism, she became an advocate for workers, the poor, and pacifism, making New York her base.

Mother Teresa (1910–1997) . . . . Macedonian-born nun who spent her life operating a home for the dying in Calcutta, India

Martin Luther King Jr. (1929–1968) . . . . Baptist minister who led the civil-rights movement; won the Nobel Peace Prize in 1966

Millard Fuller (1935–) . . . . Founder and president of the ministry Habitat for Humanity International, which provides housing for needy families worldwide

❊ ST. PATRICK'S BREASTPLATE ❊

According to legend, St. Patrick wrote this hymn on his breastplate, or *lorica*, to protect himself from an ambush, and when he and his companions passed by their enemies, they appeared to be deer. It is sometimes called the *Deer's Cry*.

I bind unto myself today
The strong Name of the Trinity,
By invocation of the same
The Three in One and One in Three.

I bind this today to me forever
By power of faith, Christ's incarnation;
His baptism in Jordan river,
His death on Cross for my salvation;
His bursting from the spicèd tomb,
His riding up the heavenly way,
His coming at the day of doom
I bind unto myself today.

I bind unto myself the power
Of the great love of cherubim;
The sweet "Well done" in judgment hour,
The service of the seraphim,
Confessors' faith, Apostles' word,
The Patriarchs' prayers, the prophets' scrolls,
All good deeds done unto the Lord
And purity of virgin souls.

I bind unto myself today
The virtues of the star lit heaven,
The glorious sun's life giving ray,
The whiteness of the moon at even,
The flashing of the lightning free,
The whirling wind's tempestuous shocks,
The stable earth, the deep salt sea
Around the old eternal rocks.

I bind unto myself today
The power of God to hold and lead,
His eye to watch, His might to stay,
His ear to hearken to my need.
The wisdom of my God to teach,
His hand to guide, His shield to ward;

The word of God to give me speech,
His heavenly host to be my guard.
Against the demon snares of sin,
The vice that gives temptation force,
The natural lusts that war within,
The hostile men that mar my course;
Or few or many, far or nigh,
In every place and in all hours,
Against their fierce hostility
I bind to me these holy powers.

Against all Satan's spells and wiles,
Against false words of heresy,
Against the knowledge that defiles,
Against the heart's idolatry,
Against the wizard's evil craft,
Against the death wound and the burning,
The choking wave, the poisoned shaft,
Protect me, Christ, till Thy returning.

Christ be with me, Christ within me,
Christ behind me, Christ before me,
Christ beside me, Christ to win me,
Christ to comfort and restore me.
Christ beneath me, Christ above me,
Christ in quiet, Christ in danger,
Christ in hearts of all that love me,
Christ in mouth of friend and stranger.

I bind unto myself the Name,
The strong Name of the Trinity,
By invocation of the same,
The Three in One and One in Three.
By Whom all nature hath creation,
Eternal Father, Spirit, Word:
Praise to the Lord of my salvation,
Salvation is of Christ the Lord.

❧ CHRISTIAN PICKUP LINES ❧

"Hi, my name's Will
. . . God's will."

"Has anyone ever told you
your eyes are like doves and
your neck is like the tower
of David?"

"I think God was showing off
when he made you."

"Nice WWJD bracelet!
'Who would Jesus date?'—uh,
I mean, 'What would Jesus do?'"

"Did I tell you my great uncle
was a personal friend of
Billy Graham?"

"Hey, baby, you wanna take the
church van for a spin?"

"So . . . what's your favorite
Bible verse?"

"That *Strong's Exhaustive
Concordance* looks pretty heavy.
Could I carry it for you to
your next class?"

"I don't see it myself, but people
tell me I look like Michael
W. Smith."

"Would you like to come over to
my place and see my collection
of C. S. Lewis books?"

❧ HOW TO BENEFIT FROM A LECTIONARY ❧

Many Christians follow a personal plan for reading through the Bible in a year, but what about the Bible passages chosen for reading in their church's worship services? Lectionaries are lists of Scripture readings to be read throughout the year in Christian worship. Believers have used lectionaries since the fourth century, but the Protestant Reformers largely abandoned them in favor of preaching straight through the books of the Bible. In the 1960s a group called the *Consultation on Common Texts* began to develop a lectionary that Catholic, Anglican, and other Protestant churches in North America could use.

The *Revised Common Lectionary* arranges the Scripture readings in a three-year cycle: A, B, and C. For each Sunday there are readings from the Old Testament, Psalms, Epistles, and Gospels, with occasional readings from the Apocrypha (an alternate Old Testament reading is supplied). Each denomination using the *Revised Common Lectionary* has its own minor variations to accommodate its special worship needs, but on a given Sunday the readings are likely to be much the same. Year A begins with the Advent season in November 2004, 2007, 2010, and so on.

Using a lectionary helps to coordinate the seasons of the church year with God's history of salvation, especially the gospel story of Christ. It also encourages preachers not to overemphasize their favorite passages while neglecting others.

❊ BIBLE RECIPES ❊

Unleavened Bread
2 cups whole wheat flour
1 tablespoon cooking oil
½ teaspoon salt

Adding enough warm water, mix the ingredients into a smooth dough. Let the mixture rest for at least a half-hour. Then roll out portions (about the size of a golf ball) on a floured board to about the size of a saucer. Place the cakes on a hot plate or skillet till they begin to blister, then turn them over and do the other side. A covered grill can also be used. Any grain flour may be substituted for wheat.

Boiled Leeks
3 large leeks
1¼ teaspoons toasted mustard seed
1 tablespoon red wine vinegar
2 tablespoons olive oil
Salt and pepper to taste

Rinse the leeks under running water. Trim the ends and cut them crosswise into 1/2-inch slices. Bring a pot of water to a boil, add the leeks, and cook 20–25 minutes until very soft. Drain, and then place in a serving dish. Finely grind 1 teaspoon of the toasted mustard seeds. Blend the vinegar and ground mustard seed. Slowly whisk in the olive oil and season with salt and pepper. Spoon this mixture over the leeks. Sprinkle the remaining 1/4 teaspoon whole mustard seeds over the leeks and serve at room temperature. Recipe serves 4.

Esau's Pottage
1 cup uncooked barley
1 cup uncooked lentils
1 large onion, chopped
½ cup celery, chopped
1 clove of garlic, minced or pressed
1 teaspoon salt

Combine all ingredients in a covered pot. Bring to a boil, then reduce heat and simmer until done (may be baked for 45 minutes at 350 degrees). Serve with bread. Recipe serves 8.

❦ HYMNS BASED ON THE PSALMS ❦

Psalm 8 . . . . "O How Glorious, Full of Wonder" (Curtis Beach, 1940s)

Psalm 19 . . . . "The Spacious Firmament on High" (Joseph Addison, 1712)

Psalm 23 . . . . "The King of Love My Shepherd Is" (Henry W. Baker, 1868)

Psalm 23 . . . . "The Lord's My Shepherd, I'll Not Want" (Scottish Psalter, 1650)

Psalm 34   "Through All the Changing Scenes of Life" (Tate and Brady, 1696)

Psalm 46 . . . . "A Mighty Fortress Is Our God" (Martin Luther, 1529)

Psalm 72 . . . . "Hail to the Lord's Anointed" (James Montgomery, 1821)

Psalm 72 . . . . "Jesus Shall Reign" (Isaac Watts, 1719)

Psalm 84 . . . . "How Lovely Is Thy Dwelling Place" (Scottish Psalter, 1650)

Psalm 87 . . . . "Glorious Things of Thee Are Spoken" (John Newton, 1779)

Psalm 90 . . . . "O God, Our Help in Ages Past" (Isaac Watts, 1719)

Psalm 97 . . . . "Rejoice, the Lord Is King" (Charles Wesley, 1744)

Psalm 98 . . . . "Joy to the World! the Lord Is Come" (Isaac Watts, 1719)

Psalm 100 . . . . "Before Jehovah's Awful Throne" (Isaac Watts, 1707)

Psalm 103 . . . . "O My Soul, Bless God the Father" (Presbyterian Book of Psalms, 1871)

Psalm 104 . . . . "O Worship the King" (Robert Grant, 1833)

Psalm 117 . . . . "From All That Dwell Below the Skies" (Isaac Watts, 1719)

Psalm 148 . . . . "Praise the Lord! O Heavens, Adore Him" (Founding Hospital Collection, 1796)

❦ THE FAMOUS WESLEYAN QUADRILATERAL ❦

The phrase *Wesleyan Quadrilateral* has come into use to denote four principal factors that John Wesley believed would help in understanding Christian faith. Many theologians take it as a good paradigm for doing theological work.

1. *Scripture* is the primary source and standard for Christian teaching.

2. *Tradition* is the witness to the development of the faith through the history of the church.

3. *Reason* is discerning, consistent thinking about the truths of the faith and its logical exposition.

4. *Experience* is the believer's living out of his or her faith.

❀ NORTH AMERICAN TOWNS WITH BIBLICAL NAMES ❀

To list all the places in North America with names from the Bible would fill several pages. We can mention only some of the most often used or interesting names and the larger cities. Bible names in Canada and the United States come in two categories: places named for people in the Bible and places named for biblical locations.

Places with names of apostles or gospel writers include

Paul—St. Paul, Alberta and KS; San Pablo, CA; South St. Paul, MN

Peter—Petersburg, VA; Pierre, SD; San Pedro, CA

Matthew—St. Matthews, KY; San Mateo, CA

Mark—San Marcos, CA and TX

Luke—Lucas, TX; Lucasville, OH. Toledo, OH, is in Lucas County.

James—Jamestown, NY, ND, and VA; St-Jacques, Quebec

John—Johnstown, NY and PA; St. Johns, MI; St. Johnsbury, VT; St-Jean, Quebec; San Juan, TX

Thomas—Thomas, WV; St. Thomas, Ontario; Thomasville, GA and NC; Thomaston, GA

Philip—Philipsburg, PA; Phillipsburg, KS

These are some other interesting names:

Babylon and West Babylon, NY

Beulah, ND

Dothan, AL

Emmaus, PA

Fair Haven, VT

Gahanna, OH

Jericho, NY and VT

Mars Hill, ME

Moab, UT

Nazareth, PA

Palestine, TX; East Palestine, OH

Paradise, CA

Philippi, WV

Pisgah, AL and OH

Rehoboth, MA; Rehoboth Beach, DE

Sardis, MS

Sidon, MS

Sodom, ME

Tekoa, WA

Zarephath, NJ

Zion and Mt. Zion, IL

A Theological Miscellany

❊ WOMEN IN THE LIFE OF PAUL ❊

Some have accused the apostle Paul of downplaying the role of women in the church, but in fact a number of women were involved in his ministry or played a part in his story. They are mentioned in his letters, in the book of Acts, or in apocryphal sources.

- Paul's mother is not mentioned in the Bible, though she must have lived in Paul's home city of Tarsus (Acts 21:39). Paul was both a Jew and a Roman citizen. His citizenship could have come from his father's status. Probably both his parents were Jewish; but if his father was not, by Jewish custom Paul would have been considered a Jew through his mother.
- Paul's sister apparently lived in Jerusalem; her son warned Paul of an ambush (Acts 23:16).
- Lydia was a businesswoman of Thyatira who provided hospitality for Paul and the apostles (Acts 16:14–15).
- A slave girl, out of whom Paul cast a spirit of divination (Acts 16:18), became the cause of a disturbance in Philippi that led to Paul's imprisonment and the salvation of the jailer and his family.
- Prisca (Priscilla) and her husband, Aquila, labored with Paul in Corinth and Ephesus, both in evangelism and in their craft of leatherworking (tentmaking), and at one point they even saved his life (Rom. 16:4).
- Phoebe was a deaconess in the church of Cenchreae, whom Paul commended to the church in Rome (Rom. 16:1).
- Mary was a hard worker in the Roman congregation (Rom. 16:6).
- Tryphaena, Tryphosa, and Persis were workers Paul knew in the church in Rome (Rom. 16:12).
- Rufus's mother was like a mother to Paul (Rom. 16:13).
- Julia and the unnamed sister of Nereus were also members of the congregation in Rome (Rom. 16:15).
- Euodia and Syntyche were fellow workers with Paul in the church in Philippi; Paul urged them to settle their quarrel, whatever it was (Phil. 4:2).
- Nympha made her house available for church gatherings, apparently in Laodicea (Col. 4:15).
- Apphia was the wife either of Philemon or Archippus, and apparently the church in Colossae met in her home (Philem. 1:2).
- Lois and Eunice were Timothy's grandmother and mother, whom Paul respected for their faith (2 Tim. 1:5).
- Thecla was said to be a girl from Iconium who broke her engagement when converted, joined Paul in his missionary work, and was martyred in her old age (apocryphal Acts of Paul).

❀ CHRISTIAN QUOTABLES ❀

"Thou hast made us for Thyself, and our hearts are restless until they find their rest in Thee." —Augustine of Hippo

"The Christian ideal has not been tried and found wanting; it has been found difficult and left untried." — G. K. Chesterton

"Worship is the normal employment of moral beings." —A. W. Tozer

"No man is a fool to exchange what he cannot keep for that which he cannot lose." —attributed in several forms to Jim Elliot

"Never forget that only dead fish swim with the stream."—Malcolm Muggeridge

"I believe in Christianity as I believe in the rising sun; not because I see it, but by it I can see all else." —C. S. Lewis

"I have had more trouble with myself than with any other man." —D. L. Moody

"Going to church doesn't make you a Christian any more than going to the garage makes you a car." — attributed to several, including Moshe Rosen and Laurence J. Peter

"There are many of us that are willing to do great things for the Lord, but few of us are willing to do little things." —D. L. Moody

"Cleanliness is indeed next to godliness." —John Wesley

"I know God will not give me anything I can't handle. I just wish that he didn't trust me so much." —Mother Teresa

"Anything worth doing is worth doing poorly."—attributed to G. K. Chesterton

"Whoever acknowledges the leading truths of Christianity, and conforms his life to that acknowledgement, we esteem a Christian." —Barton W. Stone

"If we cannot believe God when circumstances seem to be against us, we do not believe Him at all." — Charles H. Spurgeon

"If a man hasn't discovered something that he would die for, he isn't fit to live."—Martin Luther King Jr.

"Worry does not empty tomorrow of its sorrow; it empties today of its strength." —Corrie ten Boom

"Do all the good you can by all the means you can in all the places you can at all the times you can to all the people you can as long as ever you can." —John Wesley

❦ CHRISTIAN QUOTABLES—CONT. ❦

"Evidence of our hardness is that we are more concerned about our sufferings than our sins." —Matthew Henry

"My temptations have been my masters in divinity." —Martin Luther

"This life was not intended to be the place of our perfection, but the preparation for it." —Richard Baxter

"The world is my parish." —John Wesley

"Faith isn't believing what you know isn't true." —Donald T. Rowlingson

"Go into all the world and preach the gospel, and if necessary, use words."—Francis of Assisi

❦ FAMOUS MARTYRS ❦

The word *martyr* comes from a Greek word meaning "witness," and it applies to people who have died because of their Christian belief, practice, and testimony. This is a short list that includes both some slain for being Christians and some executed for advocating reform in the church. The apostle Paul and Jesus' disciples, all of whom are said to have been martyred except John, are not listed.

Stephen, the first martyr, around AD 34

Polycarp, bishop of Smyrna, around 160

Justin Martyr, apologist, around 165

Perpetua and Felicitas, women of Carthage, 203

Cyprian, bishop of Carthage, 258

George, Christian of Asia Minor, fourth century (the "great martyr" of the Eastern churches)

Thomas à Becket, archbishop of Canterbury, 1170 (the "holy blissful martyr" of Chaucer's *Canterbury Tales*)

Jan Hus, Bohemian reformer, 1415

Joan of Arc, French visionary and nationalist, 1431

William Tyndale, English Bible translator, 1536

John Philpot, English Protestant cleric, 1553

John Bradford, English Protestant scholar, 1555

Thomas Cranmer, archbishop of Canterbury, 1556

Dietrich Bonhoeffer, German theologian, 1945

Jim Elliot, American missionary to Auca Indians of Ecuador, 1956

❈ GROWTH OF MAJOR RELIGIOUS GROUPS ❈ IN THE UNITED STATES, 1650-1950

Groups are listed in order of the number of congregations in 1950. If no number appears, the movement had not been established in what is now the United States in the applicable year. Today's evangelical and Pentecostal churches were not present as denominational groups in 1850.

Denomination	1650	1750	1850	1950	Percent Growth 1850–1950
Baptist	2	132	9,375	77,000	721
Methodist			13,820	54,000	291
Lutheran	4	138	1,217	16,403	1,248
Roman Catholic	6	30	1,221	15,533	1,172
Presbyterian	4	233	4,824	13,200	174
Anglican/Episcopal	31	289	1,459	7,784	434
Christian/Disciples of Christ			1,898	7,769	309
Congregational	62	465	1,706	5,679	233
German Reformed		90	338	2,754	715
Mormon			16	2,693	16,731
Jewish		5	30	2,000	6,567
Dutch Reformed	3	79	330	763	131
Quaker	1	250	654	726	11

❈ A SHORT HISTORY OF THE CHRISTMAS TREE ❈

The origins of the Christmas tree go back to antiquity. It is said that ancient Egyptians, for example, hung green palm branches in their homes on the shortest day of the year, symbolizing the triumph of life over death. Trees that stay green all year were thought to ward off illness and evil spirits, and people hung branches over their doors and windows. The Romans used evergreens as decorations during Saturnalia, their winter festival. Druid priests decorated oak trees with apples during their celebration of the winter solstice. By the Middle Ages the custom of decorating evergreens had crept into Christian practice with the "Paradise tree," hung with apples, that was used on the Feast of Adam and Eve, December 24. A legend holds that a seventh-century English monk used the triangle-shaped fir tree to teach Germans about the Holy Trinity.

❀ A SHORT HISTORY OF THE CHRISTMAS TREE—CONT. ❀

Martin Luther is said to have decorated a small tree with candles for his children. In Strasbourg in the 1600s, trees were decorated with sweets and colored paper flowers, and tinsel began to be used in Germany. In 1714 England took on a German ruler, George I from Hanover, and German merchants living in England began to use the Christmas tree. When pictures of Queen Victoria and her German husband, Prince Albert, appeared in London newspapers, showing them with their children around a Christmas tree, the tree became fashionable in English and East Coast American society. Some of the German Hessians who fought in the Revolutionary War had remained in America and had already introduced the tree in their communities. After Queen Victoria, the use of the tree went into decline but was revived in the 1930s when Charles Dickens's writings popularized it again in Britain and North America. In Catholic countries of southern Europe, however, the crèche or manger scene has been more popular.

❀ THE "CURSING" PSALMS ❀

Some of the Psalms are called *psalms of imprecation*, or cursing, because they call upon the Lord to avenge the speaker's enemies. An example is this passage from Psalm 109:

> May his days be few;
>> may another seize his goods!
> May his children be fatherless,
>> and his wife a widow!
> May his children wander about and beg;
>> may they be driven out of the ruins they inhabit!
> May the creditor seize all that he has;
>> may strangers plunder the fruits of his toil!
> Let there be none to extend kindness to him,
>> nor any to pity his fatherless children! (vv. 8–12)

Other psalms that might be called psalms of imprecation are 35, 55, 69, 73, 79, 137; many others mention the speaker's enemies without actually calling for bad things to happen to them. When John Wesley prepared a collection of psalms for the use of American Methodists, he removed these "cursing psalms," regarding them as unfit for the lips of Christian worshipers.

The speaker in these psalms never threatens to attack his enemies himself. Instead, he appeals to God to vindicate him, for he sees himself as the Lord's servant and the Lord's enemies as his own.

❧ PHONY FEASTS AND FUNNY FESTIVALS ❧

The Feast of Fools took place around New Year's Day in France and England, during the twelfth to fourteenth centuries. Subdeacons organized the festivals, which included buffoonery and humorous mock church services. The event was sometimes called the Feast of Asses and related to Balaam's donkey (Num. 22), as well as the flight of Jesus' family into Egypt after his birth. The Feast of Fools was suppressed in the fifteenth century.

Plough Monday, the first Monday after the twelve days of Christmas, was an English festival. Plowmen blackened their faces and took their decorated plows around town asking for money, accompanied by someone costumed as "the Fool."

Mardi Gras, the day before Ash Wednesday, developed in Europe as a time of extravagance before the austerity of Lent. In New Orleans it has been carried to a modern extreme.

Hallowe'en or the Eve of All Hallows (All Saints' Day) may have originated in a "memorial day" for Christian martyrs, when worshipers dressed as saints who had given their lives for the faith. Other theories suggest Jewish or pagan origins for the day and its practices. In modern times the festival has been commercialized and, to a degree, related to imagery of satanism and the occult, and many Christian families minimize it or steer clear of it entirely.

The Grimaldi Memorial Service, or Clown Sunday, is held the first Sunday of February at Holy Trinity Church in London, England. Clowns from around the world gather in full costume to honor Joseph Grimaldi (1778–1837), the father of modern clowning.

The Hare Pie (now beef) is served—actually, tossed—each year to crowds at Hallaton in Leicestershire, England, because of a bequest made centuries ago by a woman whose life was saved when a rabbit diverted her from the path of a bull. After the pie, partyers play a game in which teams try to get three barrels across goal lines a mile apart, between Hallaton and a neighboring town.

The Christian Jugglers Association participates in events such as the Groundhog Day Jugglers' Festival.

❧ THE SEVEN DEADLY SINS ❧

The traditional list of the tendencies and traits to avoid:

1. Pride (vanity)
2. Envy
3. Gluttony
4. Lust

5. Anger (wrath)
6. Greed (avarice, covetousness)
7. Sloth

❧ THE TEN COMMANDMENTS IN THE NEW TESTAMENT ❧

Jesus referred to several commandments in Matthew 15:19: "For out of the heart come evil thoughts, murder, adultery, fornication, theft, false witness, slander." He repeated several commandments in Luke 18:20: "You know the commandments: 'Do not commit adultery, Do not kill, Do not steal, Do not bear false witness, Honor your father and mother.'" Paul listed several in Romans 13:9: "The commandments, 'You shall not commit adultery, You shall not kill, You shall not steal, You shall not covet,' and any other commandment, are summed up in this sentence, 'You shall love your neighbor as yourself.'"

"You shall have no other gods before me" *(Exod. 20:3).*

"You shall love the Lord your God with all your heart, and with all your soul, and with all your mind" (Matt. 22:37, actually quoting Deut. 6:5).

"You shall not make for yourself a graven image, or any likeness of anything that is in heaven above" (v. 4).

"They exchanged the truth about God for a lie and worshiped and served the creature rather than the Creator" (Rom. 1:25).

"You shall not take the name of the LORD your God in vain" (v. 7).

"Not every one who says to me, 'Lord, Lord,' shall enter the kingdom of heaven, but he who does the will of my Father who is in heaven" (Matt. 7:21).

"Remember the sabbath day, to keep it holy" (v. 8).

"The sabbath was made for man, not man for the sabbath; so the Son of man is lord even of the sabbath" (Mark 2:27–28).

"Honor your father and your mother" (v. 12).

"'Honor your father and mother' (this is the first commandment with a promise), 'that it may be well with you and that you may live long on the earth'" (Eph. 6:2–3).

"You shall not kill" (v. 13).

"You have heard that it was said to the men of old, 'You shall not kill; and whoever kills shall be liable to judgment.' But I say to you that every one who is angry with his brother shall be liable to judgment" (Matt. 5:21–22).

"You shall not commit adultery" (v. 14).

"You who say that one must not commit adultery, do you commit adultery?" (Rom. 2:22).

"You shall not steal" (v. 15).

"But let none of you suffer as a murderer, or a thief, or a wrongdoer, or a mischief-maker" (1 Pet. 4:15).

"You shall not bear false witness" (v. 16).

"Rob no one by violence or by false accusation, and be content with your wages" (Luke 3:14).

"You shall not covet" (v. 17).

"I should not have known what it is to covet if the law had not said, 'You shall not covet'" (Rom. 7:7).

❀ REFORMERS BEFORE THE REFORMATION ❀

Peter Waldo (died 1217) of Lyons, France, protested the worldliness of the church. His followers organized a separate movement in pockets through southern and central Europe. Despite persecution until the Reformation, the Waldensian church still exists with about fifty thousand members in Italy and Latin America.

Jan Hus (1373–1415) of Bohemia refused to stop preaching when ordered to do so, and he opposed the sale of indulgences. He was excommunicated in 1412 and burned at the stake three years later.

John Wycliffe (1329–1384), English scholar, denied the Catholic doctrine of transubstantiation (the elements of the Mass actually become the body and blood of Christ) and began translating the Bible from Latin into English.

Girolamo Savonarola (1452–1498), Dominican monk and preacher, instituted a moral reform in Florence, Italy, and denounced the corruption of the papal court; he was executed as a heretic.

❀ THE COUNTER REFORMATION ❀

The Counter Reformation was a sixteenth-century movement for reform and missionary outreach in the Roman Catholic Church, partly as a response to the Protestant Reformation. New religious orders were established to revive the ideals of charitable work and evangelism Francis of Assisi established. Chief among these was the Society of Jesus (Jesuits), founded by Ignatius Loyola and others, which became a powerful anti-Protestant force. A revival of Catholic devotion took place through the work of figures such as Teresa of Avila, John of the Cross, and Francis of Sales. The Council of Trent (1545–1563) reformed the structure of the church and reaffirmed Catholic teaching in opposition to Protestant views. The power of the papacy was strengthened and the Latin Mass was standardized to the form known in Rome, known today as the *Tridentine Mass* after the Council of Trent.

❀ THE CHRISTMAS CACTUS ❀

The Christmas cactus (*Schlumbergera bridesii* and other varieties) is native to southeastern Brazil. The scientific name comes from Frederick Schlumberger, a Belgian explorer and horticulturist, who discovered the genus in the 1800s. The Christmas cactus is not a true cactus and requires more frequent watering than its name implies. It derives its popular name from its tendency to bloom at the beginning of winter, but some varieties bloom at other times.

❧ SOME LUTHERAN BODIES IN NORTH AMERICA ❧

American Association of Lutheran Churches • Apostolic Lutheran Church of America • Association of Free Lutheran Congregations • Canadian Association of Lutheran Congregations • Church of the Lutheran Brethren of America • Church of the Lutheran Confession • Concordia Lutheran Conference • Estonian Evangelical Lutheran Church • Evangelical Catholic Church • Evangelical Community Church—Lutheran • Evangelical Lutheran Church in America • Illinois Lutheran Conference • Independent Lutheran Congregations • International Lutheran Fellowship • Laestadian Lutheran Church • Latvian Lutheran Church • Lithuanian Evangelical Lutheran Church in Diaspora • Lutheran Confessional Synod • Lutheran Congregations in Mission for Christ • Lutheran Ministerium and Synod—USA • Wisconsin Evangelical Lutheran Synod

❧ U.S. PRESIDENT WHO WAS A MINISTER ❧

James A. Garfield (1831–1881) of Ohio, the twentieth president of the United States, was a lay minister of the Disciples of Christ. He was baptized in 1850 and became a fervent preacher, though like most preachers of the Churches of Christ movement, he was never officially ordained. After serving in the Ohio Senate and the Union Army, he was elected to Congress in 1863, then to the U.S. Senate, and in 1880 was elected president.

As president, Garfield opposed the system of patronage in which U.S. senators controlled political appointments in their states. As a result, he angered many who were seeking such appointments. A disgruntled office-seeker shot Garfield in July 1881, and after lingering several months, he died in September.

❧ THE FIRST AND ONLY ENGLISH POPE . . . ❧
AND THE MAN WHO NEARLY BECAME THE SECOND

Only one pope spoke a form of English as his native language. Nicholas Brekespear reigned as Pope Adrian IV from 1154 till 1159. Another Englishman, however, came close to being elected pope. Reginald Pole, a scholar, spent most of his time in Rome and other parts of Europe, and he partially avoided being involved in the controversies over the marriages of Henry VIII. He was regarded as a favorite to succeed Pope Paul III, who died in 1549, but he had not yet been ordained a priest and did not push his own candidacy. When Mary I ("Bloody Mary") became queen of England, she had Pole ordained and made him archbishop of Canterbury, succeeding the martyred Thomas Cranmer.

❊ RELIGIOUS WORDS TURNED SECULAR ❊

Word	Original Religious Usage	Common Secular Meaning
Bedlam	A corruption of *Bethlehem*, from a London insane asylum called the Hospital of St. Mary of Bethlehem	A state of uproar or confusion
Crusade	One of a series of medieval expeditions to recover the Holy Land for Christianity	A zealous and sustained effort to achieve a goal or remedy some undesirable situation
Dogmatic	Dogmatic theology, or *dogmatics*, is the discipline that interprets the teachings of a religious faith	Asserting an opinion, often arrogantly or without sufficient evidence
Enthusiasm	Filled with religious fervor, from a Greek word based on *theos*, "God"	Strong excitement or feeling for a cause or activity
Good-bye	Shortened form of *God be with you*	Simple indication of leaving or parting
Heretic	From a Greek word meaning the action of choosing or taking; one who holds a view that contradicts established church teaching	A person who dissents from the generally accepted thinking on any subject
Kosher	Permitted by the Jewish dietary laws of *Kashrut*	Being proper, acceptable, or satisfactory
Martyr	From the Greek word for "witness"; a person who is killed for his or her religious stance	Any person who incurs loss or death for a cause or principle
Ordinary	A church official, especially a bishop, having responsibility for a specified territory or group; also the part of the Mass that does not vary with days or seasons of the liturgical year	The usual condition or course of things, i.e., "nothing out of the ordinary"; in Britain, an eating house serving set meals
Orientation	Facing or pointing toward the East or Orient; used of temples or churches where the altar is placed at the east end	Making someone familiar with an existing environment or situation, as "new member orientation," or directing something toward a particular group
Orthodox	From Greek elements meaning "correct opinion" or "right	Conforming to established or conventional ideas; a different

❧ RELIGIOUS WORDS TURNED SECULAR—CONT. ❧

Word	Original Religious Usage	Common Secular Meaning
	thinking." The term is used theologically to refer to the Eastern churches and to generally accepted Christian belief as opposed to that of splinter groups ("heterodox").	way of doing something might be called *unorthodox*
Pall	A cloth draped over a casket or a stiffened linen placed over the Communion chalice	An overspreading atmosphere of gloom or dismay
Placebo	From Latin for "I shall please," a name for the Roman Catholic vespers for the dead	Something intended to soothe, or a substance having no effect used as a control in testing medications
Proselyte	From Greek words meaning "an alien resident"; a new convert to a religious group, especially to Judaism	A person who comes to accept a new, perhaps controversial, idea
Passion	From a Latin root referring to suffering, or being acted upon; the suffering of Christ leading to the crucifixion	Enthusiasm or deep conviction for something, or romantic and erotic emotions
Pontificate	(Noun) The office or term of a pope, or *pontiff*	(Verb) To make pompous or dogmatic statements
Regular	From the Latin word for "rule"; denoting a member of a religious order that follows its particular *rule* or lifestyle	Formed or ordered according to some generally accepted pattern, arrangement, or usage; formed or functioning in a fixed or uniform way
Scapegoat	The goat driven into the wilderness on the Day of Atonement, bearing the sin of the people (Lev. 16:10)	A person punished for wrongdoing by others or made the object of hostility for no reason.
Set in stone	Refers to the giving of the Ten Commandments on stone tablets (Exod. 24:12)	Unchangeable

❋ AMERICAN RELIGIOUS MOVEMENTS ❋
STARTED BY WOMEN

Christian Science—Grew from a church founded in 1879 in Boston by Mary Baker Eddy (1821–1910) and is still based on her writings, especially *Science and Health with Key to the Scriptures* (1875)

Holiness Groups—Denominations originating in the holiness movement, such as the Church of God (Anderson, Indiana) and the Church of the Nazarene, trace their origins to Phoebe Palmer (1807–1874), a Methodist woman who began holding meetings for the promotion of holiness in New York in 1840.

International Church of the Foursquare Gospel—Incorporated by evangelist Aimee Semple McPherson (1890–1944) in 1927 in Los Angeles

Mount Sinai Holy Church of America—Founded in 1924 by Ida Robinson

Salvation Army—Founded in London in 1878 by Catherine Booth and her husband, William Booth

Seventh-Day Adventists—Formed around 1850 largely through the influence of prophetess and writer Ellen G. White (1827–1915)

Shakers—Founded in England by Mother Ann Lee (died 1784); now almost extinct

Theosophical Society—A society advocating a Hindu-like humanist philosophy, founded in 1875 in New York by Ukrainian-born Helena P. Blavatsky (1831–1891) and others. Annie Besant (1847–1933) was a later leader of the movement. The American headquarters of the Theosophical Society are located, paradoxically, in Wheaton, Illinois, a major center for Christian organizations.

❋ A WORD THAT CHANGED CHURCH HISTORY ❋

The Nicene Creed, as used in the churches of the West (Anglican, Catholic, Lutheran, and others), contains the statement, "We believe [or I believe] in the Holy Spirit, the Lord, the giver of life, who proceeds from the Father and the Son." In Latin the phrase "and the Son" is one word: *filioque.* The word was not in the original creed as it came from the councils of Nicaea and Constantinople, but churches began to add it around the time of the Third Council of Toledo (Spain) in 589. Eastern (Orthodox) churches retain the original wording, "who proceeds from the Father," period. Support for the concept of the "double procession of the Holy Ghost" is found in New Testament passages such as John 16:14, where Jesus said the Spirit "will take what is mine and declare it to you," but Orthodox theologians have objected that there must be only one "fount of divinity" in the Godhead. The *filioque* issue has never been resolved and remains a major theological factor that keeps the Eastern and Western churches from reunification.

❋ THE MYSTERIOUS "Q": FACT OR FICTION? ❋

The first three gospels—Matthew, Mark, and Luke—cover a lot of the same material about Jesus' life and ministry, while John follows its own scheme. Scholars call the first three the *synoptic Gospels*, from Greek words that mean "seeing from the same viewpoint." How do they explain the fact that Mark is missing many of Jesus' teachings that appear in Matthew and Luke, yet wherever Mark covers the same ground, his story is a bit longer? One widely held theory is that Matthew and Luke both used Mark as a source, as well as an unknown source scholars call *Q*, from the German word *Quelle*, "source." (Luke himself seemed to admit he based his work on that of others: Luke 1:1–4.) "Q" was probably not a written document, but a collection of Jesus' teachings that had been handed down by word of mouth. It's only a theory, but it looks like this:

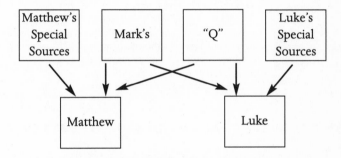

❋ MODERN MORALITY ❋

In a recent poll, Americans declared the following to be morally wrong:

Polygamy . . . . 91 percent
Married men and women having an affair . . . . 91 percent
Suicide . . . . 79 percent
Homosexual behavior . . . . 54 percent
Abortion . . . . 50 percent
Having a baby outside marriage . . . . 45 percent
Sex between an unmarried man and woman . . . . 36 percent
Buying and wearing clothing made of animal fur . . . . 31 percent
Gambling . . . . 30 percent
Death penalty . . . . 28 percent
Divorce . . . . 26 percent

❀ PROVERBS NOT FOUND IN THE BIBLE ❀

Some of these sayings may have a foundation in Scripture, and some are fragments of a biblical statement. But in these forms, they do not appear in the Bible.

Waste not, want not.
If the shoe fits, wear it.
Practice makes perfect.
Time heals all wounds.
Once saved, always saved.
Money is the root of all evil.
Cleanliness is next to godliness.
Spare the rod, and spoil the child.
You can't judge a book by its cover.
God said it, I believe it, that settles it.
God helps those who help themselves.
You can't teach an old dog new tricks.
An apple a day keeps the doctor away.
Children should be seen and not heard.
All good things come to those who wait.
If at first you don't succeed, try, try again.

❀ CHURCHES THAT WON'T USE INSTRUMENTS ❀

Early Christian worshipers did not use instruments. At first this was for practical reasons: the church was a small minority group in a hostile culture and without significant musical resources. Later on some of the church fathers justified the exclusion of instruments on theological grounds. Churches began using the organ around the seventh century, but some Protestant Reformers objected to the use of instruments in worship because they were not mentioned in the New Testament. The famous Baptist preacher C. H. Spurgeon (1834–1882) did not permit them in his church. Some groups that do not use instruments today include

- The Eastern Orthodox churches (with a few exceptions)
- The Coptic churches
- The Churches of Christ (but related groups of "Christian" churches do use instruments)
- The Reformed Presbyterian churches in North America and similar groups
- Some Quaker groups
- Primitive Baptist churches

❊ TERMS USED IN THE STUDY ❊
OF BIBLICAL MANUSCRIPTS

The study of ancient biblical manuscripts is an exacting discipline. Scholars who work with these documents and write about them use a specialized vocabulary.

Apparatus . . . . The layout of a printed edition of a text, with its footnotes and references, and the *sigla* or symbols and abbreviations (often in Latin) that indicate ancient versions, variant readings, conjectural emendations or reconstructions, other printed editions, or the various manuscript sources and their families

Codex . . . . A manuscript in book form, as opposed to a roll

Dittography . . . . An error made by repeating material while copying

Harmonization . . . . . . Similar to conflation; a copyist makes one text conform to another, e.g., inserts "missing" words in Mark by taking them from another gospel

Hand . . . . The handwriting style of a particular scribe

Lacuna . . . . A gap in the text caused by deterioration of the manuscript or other damage

Minuscule . . . . A manuscript written in a smaller cursive hand, as opposed to an uncial manuscript

Palimpsest . . . . A manuscript that has had the original writing scraped off and another text written over it. Invariably it is the older text that is of more interest to biblical scholars.

Papyrus . . . . Writing material made from reeds flattened and pressed together

Parchment . . . . Writing material made of sheepskin or goatskin

Points . . . . In a Hebrew text, the signs over, under, and within letters that represent the vowel sounds

Scripta defectiva . . . . The writing in a Hebrew or other Semitic language text in which there are no letters representing vowel sounds

Scripta plene . . . . The writing in a Hebrew text in which vowel sounds are represented by some of the consonant letters. In Hebrew there are, strictly speaking, no vowel letters, but certain consonants double as vowels in later texts.

Scriptorium . . . . A room set aside for the use of scribes or copyists

Uncial . . . . A manuscript written in all capital letters, with no word separation. The oldest New Testament manuscripts are uncials.

Vellum . . . . A fine-quality writing material made from lambskin, kidskin, or calfskin

Verso . . . . The back of a codex page, i.e., the page on the left

❄ TRADITIONAL CLERGY AND WORSHIP GARB ❄

The Geneva gown came into use for preaching during the Protestant Reformation. It is an academic garment university professors and students originally wore. It had three purposes: (1) to provide warmth in cold buildings, (2) to conceal the wearer's clothing that revealed whether he was wealthy or poor, and (3) to carry one's lunch or other items in the wide sleeves. The clerical collar was not originally a clergy garment, but something all prosperous gentlemen wore. When styles changed, the clergy were too poor to afford new clothing, and the old-style collar came to identify them. In Reformed or Anglican usage, preachers sometimes wear "preaching tabs" extending down from the collar.

Alb with cincture (cord), worn by a variety of worship leaders

Cassock, worn by clergy alone or under other vestments

Cassock with amice, worn under other vestments

Surplice with stole, over cassock

Chasuble over alb

Geneva gown with stole

Collar and Rabat (frontal or "dickey") worn by ordained clergy as everyday garb

Cotta, worn over cassock by singers or acolytes

❄ NUMBER OF LANGUAGES THE BIBLE ❄ HAS BEEN TRANSLATED INTO

The Holy Bible has been translated into at least 2,018 languages, with countless additional translations of portions of the Scriptures. There are also many recorded audio translations for unwritten languages. By comparison, the works of Shakespeare, whom many consider to be the master writer of the English language, have been translated into only 50 languages.

❧ A MOTLEY CREW: ISRAEL'S JUDGES ❧

The "judges" were not legal officials but local warriors or military leaders during a period of turmoil after the death of Joshua. The ending of the book of Judges summarizes this period: "In those days there was no king in Israel; every man did what was right in his own eyes" (Judg. 21:25). The era of the judges phased out with the rise of the prophet Samuel and the anointing of Saul, Israel's first king.

Here are descriptions of some of Israel's most colorful kingly characters.

Othniel	Delivered Israel from Cushan-rishathaim of Mesopotamia
Ehud	Was left-handed; he assassinated Eglon, the obese king of Moab, and freed Israel
Shamgar	Killed six hundred Philistines with an ox goad
Deborah	Urged Barak to throw off Israel's Canaanite masters
Gideon (Jerubbaal)	Gathered a commando force that defeated the Midianites, then turned down Israel's offer to make him king
Jair the Gileadite	Had thirty sons who rode on thirty donkeys
Jephthah	Defeated the Ammonites but had to sacrifice his daughter due to a rash vow
Ibzan of Bethlehem	Had thirty daughters
Abdon	Had forty sons and thirty grandsons
Samson	A Nazirite who turned away from his vow because of his interest in women; Delilah tricked him so that he was taken prisoner by the Philistines and blinded. In his last performance, he "brought down the house."

❧ THREE EXTRA FRUIT OF THE SPIRIT ❧ FOUND IN THE VULGATE

In Galatians 5:22–23, Paul listed the "fruit of the Spirit" in the believer's life:

love • goodness • joy • faithfulness • peace • gentleness (meekness) • patience (long-suffering) • self-control (temperance) • kindness

The Latin Vulgate of Jerome adds three more:

modesty • continence • chastity

Thomas Aquinas, the great Catholic theologian, defended twelve as the correct number on theological grounds, though the oldest Greek manuscripts have only nine.

A Theological Miscellany

❄ THE APOSTOLIC FATHERS ❄

The *Apostolic Fathers* is a collection of the very earliest Christian writings after the New Testament.

1 Clement (a letter from the Romans to the Corinthians)
2 Clement (an early Christian sermon)

The Letters of Ignatius, bishop of Antioch:

The Letter of Polycarp to the Philippians

To the Ephesians
To the Magnesians
To the Trallians
To the Romans
To the Philadelphians
To the Smyrneans
To Polycarp

The Didache (Teaching of the Twelve Apostles)
The Epistle of Barnabas
The Shepherd of Hermas
The Epistle to Diognetus
The Fragments of Papias

❄ CLASSIC ATTRIBUTES OF GOD ❄

These are some of the classic terms used in discussing the attributes of God.

Aseity . . . . God is self-existent, or pure, not being called into existence by anything else.
Impassibility . . . . God has no passions, that is, desires for what he does not have.
Immanence. . . . . God fills all space, even if he is not spatial.
Immensity . . . . God is not limited by space.
Immutability. . . . . As a perfect Being, God does not change.
Incomprehensibility. . . It is impossible for beings in God's creation to comprehend the Creator.
Infinity . . . . God cannot be encompassed or understood by finite intelligence.
Noncontingency . . . . . It is necessary that God exist; it is impossible for him not to be.
Nontemporality . . . . . . God is eternal, beyond the framework of time.
Omnipotence . . . . God has all power.
Omniscience. . . . . God knows all things.
Relatability . . . . God is related to his creation but not dependent on it.
Simplicity . . . . God has no parts into which he can be divided.
Transcendence . . . . God is beyond his creation, not part of it.
Ubiquity . . . . God is present in every place, or omnipresent.
Unity . . . . God is one; if he were more than one, the parts would lack what the other parts have.

❧ KOSHER REGULATIONS ❧

The word *kosher* comes from a Hebrew word meaning "fit" or "proper." Jewish kosher food laws are an extension of the commandment in Exodus 23:19, "You shall not boil a kid in its mother's milk" and the list of prohibited foods in Leviticus 11. These regulations are complex, and this is only a summary.

1. Only animals that chew their cud and have divided hooves may be eaten. (This rules out meat from pigs and many other animals.)

2. There are twenty-four specifically forbidden species of birds, but kosher observers usually limit fowl to chicken, turkey, duck, and goose.

3. Meat and poultry must be slaughtered in a particular way. Trained and certified slaughterers sever the trachea and esophagus with a special knife, then inspectors make sure the internal organs have no abnormalities.

4. No blood may be consumed, so before meat is eaten, the blood must be removed by salting or broiling.

5. Fish must have fins and scales that are easily removed, and they must be visible to the consumer when purchased. All shellfish are prohibited. Fish and meat must not be eaten together.

6. Meat and milk must never be cooked or eaten together, and as a safeguard they must not be prepared or served with the same equipment or dishes. A kosher kitchen must have two sets of utensils, one for meat and poultry and the other for dairy foods. Cheese must be certified to make sure it has been processed in a kosher manner.

7. Bread containing dairy ingredients cannot be eaten, since bread is served with most meals and one could accidentally eat dairy bread with a meat meal.

8. Food containing neither meat nor dairy products or processed with the same equipment is called *pareve*, and it may be eaten with either meat or dairy meals.

❧ *SELAH* IN THE PSALMS ❧

The term *selah* occurs seventy-one times in thirty-nine of the Psalms. No one is sure what it means. Some think of it as a reminder to meditate on what has been said. More likely, however, it comes from the verb *salal*, to "lift up" a song. It might indicate a place where instruments play an interlude. Or it could designate a point where free-flowing vocal and instrumental praise occurred, perhaps using a familiar refrain such as "O give thanks to the LORD, for he is good, / for his steadfast love endures for ever" (Ps. 136:1).

❊ WAYS TO SING THE PSALMS ❊

Psalm singing has been a feature of Christian worship from the beginning (Eph. 5:19), and in some Christian communities it has been the only type of music permitted in worship. These are some historic ways of singing the Psalms.

Plain Chant . . . . Psalms are sung according to conventional rules, using set "tones" or melodies. Parts are sometimes added to support or augment the melody.

Metrical Psalms . . . . Composers wrote measured tunes that could be used with the Psalms, in the local language. This sometimes required rearranging the words of Scripture in either a "close-fitting" or "loose-fitting" manner. A collection of these metrical psalms is called a *psalter*. "The Lord's My Shepherd, I'll Not Want" (Ps. 23, *Scottish Psalter* of 1650) is an example of a "loose fitting" and rhymed metrical psalm.

Anglican Chant . . . . This is a nonmetrical form of singing, in which it is not necessary to alter the form of the Bible text. The first part of a line is sung on a sustained pitch with supporting harmony, and the final syllables resolve in a short series of chords.

Psalm Paraphrase . . . . . . Isaac Watts departed from the tradition of metrical psalm singing in his *Psalms of David* of 1719. He wrote new, rhymed poetry based on the Psalms but often introduced Christ and the gospel into the text. Psalms of this type have become familiar hymns, such as "O God, Our Help in Ages Past" (Ps. 90).

Responsorial Psalms . . . . In this type of psalm singing, one verse serves as a refrain (antiphon) to be sung by the congregation, and a cantor sings the other verses. Sometimes the psalm is paraphrased.

Taizé Psalms . . . . In the latter half of the twentieth century, the ecumenical Taizé community of France introduced a simple form of singing for its own worship that has spread throughout the Christian world. Some of the texts used are from the Psalms.

Pointed Psalms . . . . Psalm texts are printed with symbolism, allowing them to be sung to a set of psalm tones in a style similar to Anglican chant. A Lutheran hymnal introduced this style in 1978.

Scripture Songs . . . . Some contemporary worship choruses or "Scripture songs" are psalm paraphrases. "Let Us Exalt His Name" by Stuart Dauermann is a version of Psalm 34.

❋ NOVELS BASED ON THE BIBLE ❋

Novelists have written hundreds of books based on biblical characters or events. The following is only a sampling of those published between 1880 and 1980.

Title	Author	Published in English
Ben-Hur: A Tale of the Christ	Lew Wallace	1880
Onesimus	Edwin Abbott	1882
Quo Vadis?	Henryk Sienkiewicz	1897
Paul of Tarsus	Robert Bird	1900
She Stands Alone: The Story of Pilate's Wife	Mark Ashton	1901
Balthazar	Anatole France (Jacques Anatole Thibault)	1909
The Tales of Jacob*	Thomas Mann	1933
Young Joseph*	Thomas Mann	1935
Joseph in Egypt*	Thomas Mann	1938
The Nazarene	Sholem Asch	1939
The Robe	Lloyd C. Douglas	1942
The Apostle	Sholem Asch	1943
The Hour of Barabbas	Otto Michael	1943
Joseph the Provider*	Thomas Mann	1944
The Big Fisherman	Lloyd C. Douglas	1948
Mary	Sholem Asch	1949
Prince of Egypt	Dorothy Clarke Wilson	1949
First the Blade	Drayton Mayrant	1950
Moses	Sholem Asch	1951
The Road to Bithynia	Frank G. Slaughter	1951
The Silver Chalice	Thomas B. Costain	1952
Salome, Princess of Galilee	Henry Denker	1953
Lot's Wife	Maria Ley-Piscator	1954
Daughter of Nazareth	Florence Marvyne Bauer	1955
The Prophet	Sholem Asch	1955
If I Forget Thee	Robert De Ropp	1956
Dear and Glorious Physician	Taylor Caldwell	1959
Pontius Pilate	Paul L. Maier	1968
Judas, My Brother	Frank Yerby	1968
Great Lion of God	Taylor Caldwell	1970
Justus	Arthur L. Lapham	1973
Lydia	Lois T. Henderson	1979

*The four novels by Thomas Mann were published together as *Joseph and His Brothers*.

❧ WOMEN EVANGELISTS ❧

Selina Hastings, Countess of Huntingdon (1707–1771)—While not a preacher herself, she used up her wealth in supporting the Methodist revival in England.

Sojourner Truth (Isabella Baumfree, 1797–1888)—Escaped slave who walked through Long Island and Connecticut preaching; she became a speaker for the abolition of slavery

Jarena Lee (1783–after 1850)—African-American widow from New Jersey who preached in the African Methodist Episcopal Church

Catherine Booth (1829–1890)—Preached along with her husband, William, and with him founded the Salvation Army and worked for improvement of conditions for the poor in England

Amanda Berry Smith (1837–1915)—African-American evangelist and temperance promoter

Maria Woodworth-Etter (1844–1924)—Holiness evangelist who pioneered in the Pentecostal revival

Aimee Semple McPherson (1890–1944)—Canadian-born, she preached the "foursquare gospel," opened Angelus Temple in California, and founded the Foursquare Gospel Church.

Kathryn Kuhlman (1907–1976)—Had a prominent healing ministry based in Pittsburgh, Pennsylvania

❧ RULES FOR THE BANNS OF MARRIAGE ❧

In Anglican, Catholic, and other churches, it is traditional to publish the *banns*, or announcement, of a forthcoming marriage in the parish. The purpose in doing so, in an earlier era, was to make sure the prospective bride and groom were not related too closely to be married. People who knew their family histories heard about the marriage in time to report any problem to the parish priest. Obtaining a marriage license is considered the equivalent of the banns, but many churches still follow the traditional procedure. These are the standard Anglican procedures:

1. The banns must be published in an audible manner in the parish church on three Sundays before the marriage. (Today the banns are often printed in the church bulletin.)

2. If the persons being married live in different parishes, the banns must be published in both.

3. The clergyman must be notified at least seven days before the first announcement is to be made.

4. If the couple delays marriage more than three months, the banns must be published again.

❋ THREE VIEWS OF THE MILLENNIUM ❋

Theologians offer diverging pictures of "last days" or end-time events, usually described as *millennial* views. The term *millennium* is derived from Latin for "thousand years," a period mentioned in Revelation 20. The differing views are often labeled depending on how the timing of Christ's return (his second coming or second advent) is related to this thousand-year period.

1. *Premillennialism*—Christ returns before the millennium to inaugurate it as his kingdom. Most premillennialists look for a seven-year period of "tribulation" or cataclysmic events preceding the appearance of Christ. There are subcategories of premillennialism, based on the timing of the "rapture" or "catching up" of Christians suggested in 1 Thessalonians 4:17: (a) *Pretribulationism*—the church is raptured before the Tribulation; (b) *Posttribulationism*—the church is raptured after the Tribulation; (c) *Midtribulationism*—the church is raptured during the Tribulation. This view came to the forefront among evangelicals beginning around 1900.

2. *Postmillennialism*—The millennium is a period of righteousness, peace, and blessing brought about by the steady advance of the gospel of Christ and the growing influence of the principles of God's kingdom. At the end of the millennium, Christ returns for the general resurrection and judgment. This view has been common in historic Protestant denominations.

3. *Amillennialism*—The term means "nonmillennialism." In this view, the millennium is a symbolic concept that describes the present rule of Christ through his Word and Spirit in the church. The "last days" began with Jesus' resurrection and ascension, and the "tribulation" refers to the events of the first century that led to the destruction of Jerusalem and its temple. Christ will return for judgment after his present reign, but believers enter the kingdom through new life in Christ now and at their death. This is the "classic" view that the majority of theologians held until the nineteenth century.

❋ METHODIST DENOMINATIONS IN THE UNITED STATES ❋

African Methodist Episcopal Church • African Methodist Episcopal Zion Church • Christian Methodist Episcopal Church • Congregational Methodist Church • Evangelical Methodist Church • Free Methodist Church of North America • Independent Methodist Churches • Primitive Methodist Church in the USA • Southern Methodist Church • United Methodist Church • The Wesleyan Church (originally Wesleyan Methodist Church, merged with Pilgrim Holiness Church)

❄ MANY NAMES FOR "MEN OF THE CLOTH" ❄

ARCHDEACON—A deacon who assists the bishop or who has a leading position among the other deacons of a group of churches

BISHOP—Often applied to the local pastor in Pentecostal or African-American churches

BROTHER—In Pentecostal churches, a form of address for a pastor, as in "Brother Jukes is our preacher today"; also used for respected laymen

DEACON—As a title for ordained clergy, it can designate (1) a person in process toward the priesthood or fully ordained ministry, or (2) a permanent deacon with particular assignments in the church. In some churches deacons have specific roles in the liturgy, such as reading the gospel lesson, preparing the altar for Communion, or pronouncing the dismissal.

CANON—A clergyman on the staff of a cathedral; the canons collectively are called a *chapter*

DEAN—The head of a cathedral chapter or a priest appointed as leader of a group of churches within a diocese (deanery)

DOMINIE—Traditional Dutch Reformed title for a minister

FATHER—Respectful address for a priest but not universal among Anglicans

INCUMBENT—Anglican term for the priest of a particular parish

MINISTER—General term for a clergyman but used less often in evangelical churches, and used in the Catholic Church mostly for laypeople who assist in serving Holy Communion

MONSIGNOR—Traditional title of honor conferred on a veteran Catholic priest

MR.—In classic Episcopal or other Protestant usage, the proper form of address or reference for a clergyman, i.e., "This is Mr. Bottomly, our curate."

PASTOR—Its use as a title and form of address for a local clergyman is favored in Lutheran and many evangelical and Pentecostal churches. Where not used as a form of address or title, it can designate the chief clergyman of any local church, i.e., the main priest of a Catholic parish is its pastor.

PREACHER—Often used synonymously with pastor in evangelical and Pentecostal churches

❧ MANY NAMES FOR "MEN OF THE CLOTH"—CONT. ❧

PREACHING ELDER—Title given to the main pastor or preacher in a "Christian" or "Churches of Christ" congregation

PRIEST—In the Catholic, Orthodox, or Anglican communities, a fully ordained clergy person who is authorized to preside at the Eucharist

RECTOR—Anglican or Episcopal title for the head pastor of a local parish

REVEREND—Strictly speaking, not a title but an honorific adjective. It is not correct to say "Reverend Crawford" but "the Reverend Mr. Crawford" (or "Dr." if applicable).

TEACHING ELDER—In Presbyterian usage, an elder who is a clergyman in contrast to a lay or "ruling" elder

VICAR—In Anglican usage, the pastor of a local parish; strictly speaking, it applies to the pastor of a parish that is under the direct supervision of the bishop for whom the local clergyman acts vicariously.

❧ CRUCIFIXION SURVIVOR ❧

Crucifixion was an agonizing, prolonged method of executing people considered threats to Roman rule.

A man survived the cross some forty years after the death of Christ, during the Jewish Revolt against Rome. The Jewish historian Flavius Josephus (AD 37–100), who had gone over to the Roman side, described how this happened.

> And when I was sent by Titus Caesar with Cerealins, and a thousand horsemen, to a certain village called Thecoa, in order to know whether it were a place fit for a camp, as I came back, I saw many captives crucified, and remembered three of them as my former acquaintance. I was very sorry at this in my mind, and went with tears in my eyes to Titus, and told him of them; so he immediately commanded them to be taken down, and to have the greatest care taken of them, in order to their recovery; yet two of them died under the physician's hands, while the third recovered. (*The Life of Flavius Josephus*, chapter 75)

We don't know this survivor's name or what happened to him afterward. But he lived because the right person—his friend—happened to find him and his companions.

❦ ARAMAIC AND HEBREW WORDS ❦
IN THE NEW TESTAMENT

Aramaic, the language of some parts of the Old Testament (portions of Daniel and Ezra), is a sister language of Hebrew. It was the ordinary language of Judea and Galilee in the first century, and it is sometimes called "Hebrew" in the New Testament. Jesus probably could speak some Greek, as there were Greek-speaking cities in Galilee, and he conversed with a Greek-speaking Syrophoenician woman (Mark 7:24–30). Since Jesus mainly taught the common people, though, Aramaic was his language and that of the earliest Christians.

Some Aramaic words are preserved in the Greek New Testament:

abba	Father
akeldama	"field of blood," perhaps a proper name (Acts 1:19)
Eloi, Eloi, lama sabachthani	"My God, my God, why have you forsaken me?" (Mark 15:34, after Ps. 22:1)
ephphatha	"Be opened" (Mark 7:34)
korbanas	The temple treasury (Matt. 27:6)
mammonas	"Mammon," "riches" (Matt. 6:24)
maranatha	"Our Lord has come" or "Our Lord, come!" (1 Cor. 16:22)
talitha koumi	"Little girl, arise!" (Mark 5:41)
rabbi	"My Master" or "My great one" (rabboni in John 20:16)
raca	"You fool" (Matt. 5:22)

Other words are actually Hebrew, though transmitted through Aramaic:

Alleluia	"Praise Yahweh"
amen	"Truly, reliably"
korban	"Dedicated offering" (Mark 7:11)
pascha	Passover
geenna	Gehenna, from *gei hinnom*, or Valley of Hinnom, the Jerusalem city dump
manna	Manna, literally, "What is it?"
sabaoth	From Hebrew meaning "hosts, armies" (Rom. 9:29; James 5:4)
sabbaton	Sabbath
satanas	Satan, or "the adversary"

❅ POPULAR HYMNS OF CHARLES WESLEY ❅

Charles Wesley (1707–1788) wrote more than six thousand hymns. These are some of the ones most often sung today.

"And Are We Yet Alive" (1749)

"And Can It Be That I Should Gain?" (1738)

"Blow Ye the Trumpet, Blow" (1750)

"A Charge to Keep I Have" (1762)

"Christ the Lord Is Risen Today" (1739)

"Christ, Whose Glory Fills the Skies" (1740)

"Come, Holy Ghost, Our Hearts Inspire" (1740)

"Come, Let Us Join Our Friends Above" (1759)

"Come, O Thou Traveler Unknown" (1742)

"Come, Sinners, to the Gospel Feast" (1747)

"Come, Thou Long Expected Jesus" (1744)

"Forth in Thy Name, O Lord, I Go" (1749)

"Hark, the Herald Angels Sing" (1739)

"How Can a Sinner Know?" (1749)

"How Happy Every Child of Grace (1759)"

"I Know That My Redeemer Lives" (1741)

"Jesus, Lover of My Soul" (1740)

"Jesus! the Name High over All" (1749)

"Jesus, Thine All-Victorious Love" (1740)

"Jesus, United by Thy Grace" (1740)

"Love Divine, All Loves Excelling" (1747)

"O Come and Dwell in Me" (1762)

"O for a Heart to Praise My God" (1742)

"O for a Thousand Tongues to Sing" (1739)

"O Thou Who Camest from Above" (1762)

"Rejoice, the Lord Is King" (1744)

"Sing to the Great Jehovah's Praise" (1750)

"Talk with Us, Lord" (1740)

"Thou Hidden Source of Calm Repose" (1749)

"'Tis Finished! The Messiah Dies" (1762)

"Where Shall My Wondering Soul Begin?" (1739)

"Ye Servants of God, Your Master Proclaim" (1744)

❧ CATHOLIC SAINTS OF THE TWENTIETH CENTURY ❧

The Catholic Church has canonized (declared saints) at least twenty-four people who lived in the twentieth century. Among them:

Pope Pius X . . . . Giuseppe Melchiorre Sarto (1835–1914) reformed the liturgy, fought Modernism, reorganized the Roman curia, and otherwise encouraged renewal in the church. Canonized by Pope Pius XII in 1954.

Frances Xavier Cabrini . . . . . . Known as Mother Cabrini, she founded Missionaries (1850–1917) of the Sacred Heart with clinics and homes in New York, Latin America, and elsewhere. Canonized by Pope Pius XII in 1946.

Teresa de los Andes . . . . Juana Fernandez Solar, a nun, the first Chilean to be (1900–1920) declared a saint. Canonized by Pope John Paul II in 1993.

Ivan Merz (1896–1928). . . . . . Croatian layman who took a vow of celibacy and worked for evangelism and revival in the church. Canonized by Pope John Paul II in 2003.

László Batthyány- . . . . Hungarian physician who turned an inherited family Strattmann (1870–1931) castle into a hospital for the poor. Canonized in 2003 by Pope John Paul II.

Maximilian Kolbe . . . . Raymond Kolbe, Polish Franciscan priest who was (1894–1941) executed at Auschwitz. Canonized by Pope John Paul II in 1982.

Teresa Benedicta of . . . . Edith Stein, convert from Judaism who became a the Cross (1891–1942) nun and died in the Auschwitz gas chambers. Canonized by Pope John Paul II in 2003.

Katharine Drexel . . . . American nun who founded the Sisters of the (1858–1955) Blessed Sacrament for work among Native Americans and African-Americans. Canonized by Pope John Paul II in 2000.

Maria of Jesus Crucified . . . . Croatian nun who founded the Congregation of the Petkovic (1892–1966) Daughters of Mercy. Canonized by Pope John Paul II in 2003.

❧ FAMOUS LAST WORDS ❧

Stephen, AD 36
Lord, do not hold this sin against them.

St. Lawrence (martyr), 258
Turn me. I am roasted on one side.

Thomas à Becket, 1170
I commend myself to God, the Blessed Mary, St. Denis, and the patron saints of this Church . . . Father, into your hands I commend my spirit.

Jan Hus, 1415
O, holy simplicity!

Joan of Arc, 1431
Hold the cross high so I may see it through the flames!

Martin Luther, 1546
Father, into your hands I commit my spirit; you have redeemed me, O Lord, God of truth.

Hugh Latimer, 1555
Be of good comfort, Master Ridley, and play the man; we shall this day, by God's grace, light such a candle in England as I trust shall never be put out.

Thomas Cranmer, 1556
I see Heaven open and Jesus on the right hand of God.

Cotton Mather, 1728
Is this dying? Is this all? Is this what I feared when I prayed against a hard death? Oh, I can bear this! I can bear this!

Susanna Wesley, 1742
Children, when I am gone, sing a song of praise to God.

Selina Hastings, Countess of Huntingdon, 1771
My work is done; I have nothing to do but go to my Father.

John Wesley, 1791
The best of all: God is with us!

Catherine Booth, 1890
The waters are rising, but so am I. I am not going under, but over. Do not be concerned about dying. Go on living well; the dying will be right.

Dwight L. Moody, 1899
This is my coronation day. If this is death, it is sweet!

❧ BIBLE STORIES YOU KNOW AND LOVE— ❧
AS SEEN ON THE BIG SCREEN

Joseph in the Land of Egypt (1914) • *The Chosen Prince* or *The Friendship of David and Jonathan* (1917) • *Lot in Sodom* (1933) • *Samson and Delilah* (1949) • *Quo Vadis?* (1912, 1932, 1951) • *David and Bathsheba* (1951) • *Demetrius and the Gladiators* (1954 sequel to *The Robe*) • *The Ten Commandments* (1923, 1956) • *Ben-Hur* (1907, 1925, 1959) • *The Big Fisherman* (1959) • *Solomon and Sheba* (1959) • *Esther and the King* (1960) • *Barabbas* (1961) • *Sodom and Gomorrah* (1962) • *The Bible* (1966) • *King David* (1985) • *A.D.* (1985 miniseries) • *The Prince of Egypt* (1998) • *Abraham* (TV, 1994) • *Jacob* (TV, 1994) • *David* (TV, 1997) • (See also *Jesus Goes to Hollywood: Movies about the Life of Christ*)

❀ THE TRADITIONAL SECTIONS ❀
OF A CHURCH BUILDING

Churches vary in architectural style, but these are some terms applied to the parts of a traditional church.

Altar—The table where the Mass or Eucharist is consecrated. In Protestant churches with a different theology, the proper term is *Communion table*. In evangelistic churches, the term *altar* may refer to the area at the foot of the chancel where worshipers kneel for prayer.

Ambo—A stand that combines the functions of pulpit and lectern; from the Latin prefix meaning "both." Often the ambo is called a *pulpit*.

Ambulatory—In a larger church, the area surrounding the altar where worshipers can walk; from a Latin word that refers to walking

Apse—A semicircular area in some churches where the altar is placed, projecting from the wall of the church. This end of the church is called the *east*, regardless of the actual geographical positioning of the building.

Chancel—The area from which the worship service is led. A chancel with a pulpit on one side, a lectern on the other, and the altar or Communion table in the center is sometimes called a *divided chancel*.

Choir—One of the "arms" of a cross-shaped ("cruciform") church, where the singers originally sat; if not a cruciform

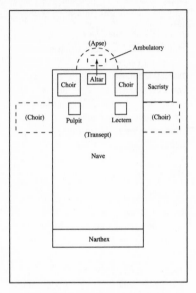

church, the choirs may be at the sides of the chancel.

Lectern—A stand for reading the Scriptures

Narthex—An area behind the nave, leading to the outside doors

Nave—The area where the congregation sits or stands; from the Latin word for "ship" because it resembles the upside-down hold of a sailing vessel. The side opposite the pulpit is called the *Gospel side*, and the side opposite the lectern is called the *Epistle side*. In churches that focus on preaching, the nave is sometimes called the *auditorium*.

❧ THE TRADITIONAL SECTIONS ❧
OF A CHURCH BUILDING—CONT.

Prayer-desk—Also called a *prie-dieu* (French for "pray God"), placed in the chancel for the use of worship leaders

Pulpit—The stand from which the sermon is preached

Sacristy—A room where the sacrament (Eucharist, Communion) is prepared; also used for vesting of clergy and others if there is no separate vestry

Sanctuary—The area around the altar, from the Latin word for "holy." In Protestant usage the term is often applied to the entire worship space, synonymous with *auditorium*.

Transept—In a cross-shaped church, the area where the arms come together; also applied to the projecting areas on either side (see *Choir*)

Vestry—A separate room where clergy or other worship functionaries put on their vestments (robes); in some churches the term refers to a fellowship hall, often in the basement.

❧ HISTORIC CHURCH CONFESSIONS ❧

In addition to the ancient creeds of the church (Apostles', Chalcedonian, Nicene, Athanasian), Protestant groups have formulated historic confessions, or statements of faith. These confessions reveal the issues churches were dealing with at various times and guide theological discussion up to the present. These are some of the historic confessions.

AUGSBURG CONFESSION (1531)—This confession, largely the work of Philipp Melanchthon, is a moderate statement of essential Lutheran doctrines such as justification by faith, with an appeal for correction of abuses in the Catholic Church.

BELGIC CONFESSION (1561)—This Reformed confession was originally drawn up in French as a repudiation of Anabaptist teachings. It was adopted as authoritative for the Netherlands in 1566 and reaffirmed by the Synod of Dort (Dordrecht) in 1619.

HEIDELBERG CATECHISM (1563)—This confession was drawn up in Heidelberg as a standard for the Palatinate, a German state.

❧ HISTORIC CHURCH CONFESSIONS—CONT. ❧

THE THIRTY-NINE ARTICLES (1571)—This document was finalized during the reign of Elizabeth I as a statement of the position of the Church of England on major theological issues of the time.

WESTMINSTER CONFESSION (1648)—This is the major confession of the Presbyterian churches, formulated by the Westminster Assembly of Divines (theologians) and ratified by the English Parliament during the Puritan Commonwealth.

SAVOY DECLARATION (1658)—This is a reaffirmation of most of the Westminster Confession, but it adds a "platform of discipline" affirming the congregational form of church government.

DECLARATION AND ADDRESS (1809)—A statement Thomas Campbell composed that advocated "simple evangelical Christianity, free from all mixture of human opinions and inventions of men."

BARMEN DECLARATION (1934)—This declaration, written largely by theologian Karl Barth (1886–1968), was issued by a group of Protestant leaders in response to the "German-Christian" movement, which was trying to reconcile the understanding of the church with conditions during the Hitler era.

❧ PROTESTANT "SAINTS" OF ❧ THE TWENTIETH CENTURY

All faithful Christians are "saints," or people called to be set apart as God's (1 Cor. 1:2). Therefore Protestants have no official process or agency to recognize anyone as a special saint. In the history of the Reformation, however, some have been widely recognized as martyrs, or witnesses who died for the faith, through such media as John Foxe's *Book of Martyrs* (first published in 1563). A list of twentieth-century saints in the Protestant community is subjective but could include the following. (Not everyone would agree with this list of Protestant "saints," and the list includes no living people.)

Czar Nicholas II .... In 2000, the Russian Orthodox declared the last czar a saint and martyr. Nicholas and the Romanov family were executed by revolutionaries in 1918.

❧ PROTESTANT "SAINTS" OF ❧
THE TWENTIETH CENTURY—CONT.

George Fox and .... Two of the four chaplains who gave their life jackets to
Clark Poling   others when their troop ship, the *Dorchester*, was torpe-
                            doed in 1943

The ten Booms   A Dutch family who hid Jewish people in their home dur-
                            ing the Nazi era. They were arrested in 1944. Casper, the
                            father, died in prison; and Betsie, a daughter, died in the
                            Ravensbruck concentration camp. Her sister Corrie
                            (1892–1983) was released and emigrated to the United
                            States, where she became influential for evangelism
                            through her writings. Willem, a brother, was arrested for
                            working with the Dutch underground and died shortly
                            after the end of World War II. Christaan, a nephew, died
                            in prison for working with the underground.

Dietrich Bonhoeffer .... German theologian executed by the Nazis
(1906–1945)

Amy Carmichael ...... Native of Ireland, sent by a Church of England missionary
(1867–1951)   society to India, where she served fifty-six years without
                            a furlough

Jim Elliot .... American missionary slain by Ecuadorian Indians
(1927–1956)

Albert Schweitzer ...... Theologian and musician who gave up a successful
(1875–1965)   European career to serve as a medical missionary in
                            Africa

Martin Luther King .... Baptist minister who led the civil-rights movement from a
(1929–1968)   Christian perspective and was assassinated

Janani Luwum .... Anglican archbishop of Uganda, who with many other
(1922–1977)   Christians withstood the dictator Idi Amin and was
                            executed

Richard Wurmbrand .... Romanian pastor and convert from Judaism, who was
(1909–2001)   tortured and imprisoned by the Communist govern-
                            ment; then after his release he led the effort in America
                            to publicize the plight of Christians in the Soviet bloc

❊ HERETICS AND THEIR HERESIES ❊

These are some of the views the majority of the Christian church judged heretical through history, even though the church did not expressly condemn all of them as such.

Movement	Major Figure	Major Idea
Montanism elite	Montanus (second century AD)	True Christians are Spirit-filled ascetics awaiting the imminent return of Christ. Tertullian (160–220), the first Christian theologian to write in Latin, was a Montanist.
Manicheism	Mani (216–276)	This was not a Christian heresy but a Gnostic sect based on the conflict between light and darkness. Jesus is the releaser of the Light imprisoned in matter.
Adoptianism	Paul of Samosata (third century AD)	Jesus was energized by the Spirit at baptism and called to be the Son of God, and in this sense only he is God. Also called Adoptianist Monarchianism.
Sabellianism	Sabellius (third century AD)	God reveals himself at different times in different modes: Father, Son, and Spirit; he cannot be all three and still be one. Also called Modalistic Monarchianism and Patripassianism; forerunner of Unitarianism.
Arianism	Arius (250–336)	The Son is subordinate to the Father; being "begotten," he had a beginning and is not coeternal with the Father.
Donatism	Donatus (died 355)	The church must be holy: those who renounce the faith under persecution cannot administer the sacraments, and converts from the Catholic Church must be rebaptized.
Apollinarianism	Apollinarius (310–390)	Christ had one will, that of the divine Word; he was fully God but not fully human.

❧ HERETICS AND THEIR HERESIES—CONT. ❧

Movement	Major Figure	Major Idea
Pelagianism	Pelagius (383–410)	People are responsible for their deeds, not predestined to them, and must take the first steps toward their own salvation.
Eutychianism	Eutyches (378–454)	Christ had only one nature, the divine. This view is called Monophysitism, and it is the doctrine of several ancient churches still in existence.
Monothelitism	Pope Honorius I (died 638)	Christ has a divine and human nature but only one "energy" or will; several figures were involved in this ongoing controversy that was more political than theological.
Socinianism	Fausto Sozzini (1539–1604)	Scripture is to be studied rationally; Christ is human, not divine. Forerunner of Unitarianism.

❧ OTHER "GODS" MENTIONED IN THE BIBLE ❧

This is a selection from the approximately fifty false gods mentioned in Scripture.

"God"	Nationality	Selected Reference	Comments
Amon	Egyptian	Jeremiah 46:25	National god of Egypt
Artemis (Diana)	Lydian	Acts 19:35	Fertility goddess
Astarte (Ishtar, Ashtoreth)	Phoenician, Canaanite	1 Kings 11:5	Goddess of evening star (Venus)
Ba'al	Canaanite	1 Kings 19:18	Means "Master, Husband"; chief god of Canaanites, paired with Ashtoreth
Ba'al-Zebul (Ba'al-Zebub)	Philistine (Ekron)	2 Kings 1:2	Name later applied to Satan (Matt. 10:25)

❊ OTHER "GODS" MENTIONED IN THE BIBLE—CONT. ❊

"God"	Nationality	Selected Reference	Comments
Bel (Marduk)	Babylonian	Isaiah 46:1	National sun god
Castor and Pollux	Greek, Roman	Acts 28:11	Twins, patron gods of sailors
Chemosh	Moabite	Numbers 21:29	Worshiped with child sacrifice
Dagon	Philistine	Judges 16:23–24	Known also in Babylonia and Canaan
Hadad	Syrian	1 Kings 15:18	Another name for Ba'al and Rimmon; worshiped throughout ancient Near East
Hermes (Mercury)	Greek	Acts 14:12	God of eloquence, good luck, divine messenger
Lilith	Semitic	Isaiah 34:14 (NRSV)	A night demon or hag
Marduk (Merodach)	Babylonian	Jeremiah 50:2	Chief god of Babylon
Moloch (Molech, Milcom)	Ammonite	2 Kings 23:10	Worshiped with human sacrifice
Nergal	Mesopotamian	2 Kings 17:30	Lord of the underworld
Queen of Heaven	Assyrian	Jeremiah 7:18	Goddess of fertility, known as Astarte or Ishtar
Rimmon	Syria	2 Kings 5:18	God of storm, equivalent to Hadad and Ba'al
Zeus (Jupiter)	Greek, Roman	Acts 14:12	Head of the Greek and Roman gods

❧ 107 "SEVENS" FOUND IN THE BIBLE ❧

Here are 107 things in the Bible said to come in groups of seven.

1. Days of creation

2. Days between Noah's dove releases

3. People spared in the flood besides Noah (2 Pet. 2:5)

4. Lambs Abraham sent to Abimelech

5. Years Jacob served Laban for Leah and Rachel

6. Times Jacob bowed to Esau

7. Fat and thin cattle in Joseph's dream

8. Ears of good and blighted corn

9. Years of plenty and famine

10. Days Joseph's family mourned for Jacob

11. Daughters of Reuel

12. Days of the Feast of Unleavened Bread

13. Lamps on the lampstand (menorah)

14. Days to make atonement

15. Times to sprinkle blood for atonement

16. Times to anoint the altar to consecrate it

17. Days Aaron is to stay in the tent for his consecration

18. Days a woman is to be unclean after bearing a male child

19. Days a leprous person is to be confined

20. Days a cleansed leper is to stay outside his tent

21. Days a newborn animal must live before it can be offered

22. Weeks between Passover and Pentecost

23. Lambs sacrificed on Pentecost

24. Days to live in shelters during the Feast of Tabernacles

25. "Weeks of years" between jubilee years

26. Altars and sacrificial animals Balaam told Balak to provide

27. Nations Israel is to displace in Canaan

28. Years between release of debts

29. Days the Israelites marched around Jericho

30. Times they marched the seventh day

31. Priests with horns who led them

32. Years Israel served Midian

33. Years Ibzan judged Israel

34. Locks of Samson's hair

35. Months the Philistines kept the ark

36. Days Saul was to wait for Samuel at Gilgal

37. Sons of Jesse that Samuel didn't choose as king

38. Days the people of

❈ 107 "SEVENS" FOUND IN THE BIBLE—CONT. ❈

Jabesh-Gilead fasted
after Saul's death

39. Sons and grandsons
of Saul hanged by
the Gibeonites

40. Years David ruled in
Hebron

41. Years it took Solomon
to build the temple

42. Days of feasting
when the temple was
dedicated

43. Days Zimri reigned
as king of Israel

44. Times Elijah told his
servant to look for
rain clouds

45. Days the kings of
Judah, Israel, and
Edom marched to
meet the Syrians

46. Times the
Shunammite's son
sneezed when return-
ing to life

47. Times Naaman
dipped in the Jordan

48. Years of famine dur-
ing Elisha's time

49. Age of Jehoash when
he began to reign

50. Sons of Elioenai

51. Kinsmen of Joel,
chief of the Gaddites

52. Counselors of
Artaxerxes

53. Days of feasting
when Ezra read the
law in the Water
Gate

54. Days of feasting
given by Ahasuerus

55. Eunuchs of
Ahasuerus

56. Princes of Persia and
Media

57. Maids given to
Esther in Ahasuerus's
harem

58. Sons of Job

59. Days and nights Job's
friends sat with him
without speaking

60. Bulls and rams Job
was told to offer for
his friends

61. Times the best silver
was purified

62. Times during the day
the psalmist praises
the Lord

63. Things that are an
abomination to the
Lord

64. Pillars of wisdom

65. Times a righteous
man falls and rises

66. Wise men a sluggard
thinks he is wiser than

67. Abominations in the
heart of the hateful

68. Women who will
cling to one man in
the day of the Lord's
judgment

69. Channels into which
the Lord will divide
the River

70. Aspects of the Spirit
of the Lord (Isa. 11:2)

71. Men of the king of
Judah's council taken
to Babylon

72. Days Ezekiel sat by
the river Chebar
before the word of
the Lord came to him

73. Years it will take
Israel to burn the
weapons of Gog and
Magog

74. Months it will require

to bury the dead of Gog and Magog

75. Steps up to the East Gate in Ezekiel's vision of the restored temple

76. Cubits in height for the inner room of the temple

77. Days to make atonement for the altar

78. Days a person is defiled after touching a dead family member

79. Times hotter than usual that Nebuchadnezzar had the furnace heated

80. Time periods through which Nebuchadnezzar is to be like an animal

81. Weeks from the proclamation to rebuild Jerusalem till the coming of the anointed one

82. Shepherds to be raised up against the Assyrian

83. Facets of the stone

set before the high priest Joshua

84. Eyes of the Lord ranging through the earth

85. Evil spirits brought back by the one cast out

86. Loaves of the boy with the loaves and fish

87. Baskets taken up after the feeding of the four thousand

88. Times Peter wondered whether he should forgive

89. Sadducee brothers who died after being married successively to the same woman

90. Demons cast out of Mary Magdalene

91. Years Anna had lived with her husband before he died

92. Times a day Jesus' disciples are to forgive a brother's sin

93. Men appointed to serve in the early church (deacons)

94. Sons of the priest Sceva

95. Days Paul stayed in Troas

96. Days Paul stayed in Tyre before going to Jerusalem

97. Days of Paul's vow of purification

98. Days Paul and Luke stayed in Puteoli before going to Rome

99. Churches of the Revelation

100. Golden lampstands

101. Stars

102. Spirits of God

103. Horns and eyes

104. Thunders

105. Seals

106. Heads of the beast

107. Bowls of wrath

❀ SIX LATIN PHRASES YOU NEED TO KNOW ❀

Sola fide, sola gratia, sola Scriptura . . . . . . "Faith alone, grace alone, Scripture alone," the watchwords of the Protestant Reformation

Ecce homo . . . . "Behold the man," the words of Pilate in John 19:5. The traditional site in Jerusalem is called the *Ecce Homo Arch.*

In hoc signo vinces . . . . "In this sign you will conquer," words the Roman emperor Constantine reportedly saw in the sky, together with a cross, which led to his conversion to Christianity

Soli Deo gloria . . . . "To God alone be the glory"; some Christian composers would write these words on their manuscripts

Fides quaerens intellectum . . . . "Faith in search of understanding." The phrase goes back to the work of Thomas Aquinas, the greatest medieval Catholic theologian; it refers to the idea that, while working from a nonnegotiable commitment of faith, we still seek to understand reality and truth through all avenues of inquiry.

Ex nihilo . . . . "From nothing," the thought that a new reality has come about having no previous form of existence; it is applied to God's creation of the universe

❀ OBSCURE CHRISTIAN "ISMS" ❀

Annihilationism . . . . The view that those who are not "saved" are not eternally punished, but simply cease to exist

Antidisestablishmentarianism . . . . The movement opposing those who advocated withdrawing state sponsorship from the Church of England

❀ OBSCURE CHRISTIAN "ISMS"—CONT. ❀

Antinomianism . . . . The view that Christians are free from any obligation to hold to a moral law

Dispensationalism . . . . A system in which Bible history is divided into periods during which God relates in a different way to the course of events. A cornerstone of the system is the idea that the age of the church is an interruption in God's plan for Israel, which will resume after the church is removed.

Docetism . . . . A semi-Christian form of Gnosticism (see below) holding that Christ, a spiritual being, appeared only to experience physical existence and death

Dualism . . . . A philosophy holding that the spiritual and material, or good and evil, are separate realities with opposing origins; contrasted with monism

Erastianism . . . . The doctrine that the civil authorities or legislators of a state are empowered to make decisions about the state's established religion, even if they are not adherents of it

Exemplarism . . . . The view that Christ's death atones for sin by setting a moral example that encourages repentance

Fideism . . . . The doctrine that the knowledge of divine matters can be attained only by faith, not the intellect

Gnosticism . . . . Derived from the Greek word for knowledge, this term describes a tendency that took many forms but essentially refers to a system in which salvation comes from receiving knowledge of matters hidden from others. Gnosticism sharply distinguishes the superior spiritual from the inferior material.

❈ OBSCURE CHRISTIAN "ISMS"—CONT. ❈

Iconoclasm . . . . The movement against the veneration of images of the divine, and the effort to destroy these images

Infralapsarianism . . . . A form of the doctrine of predestination that holds that God's decrees as to who would be the "elect" occurred after the fall of man; contrasted with supralapsarianism

Latitudinarianism . . . . A policy of retaining conventional church practices while deemphasizing matters of dogma, church organization, or worship issues. Today it might be called "cutting people some slack."

Modernism . . . . The adoption of a "modern" perspective on questions of truth, including a critical approach to the Bible, an emphasis on Christian life and society rather than doctrine, and the view that today's church is evolving into a reality not dependent on its ancient origins

Monism . . . . A philosophy that tries to explain everything that exists in terms of a single reality; contrasted with dualism or pluralism

Nominalism . . . . The philosophy that abstract categories of things, or "universals," are only names (*nomina*), and the reality is in the things themselves; contrasted with realism

Paedobaptism . . . . The practice of baptizing children as well as adults

Pluralism . . . . Similar to dualism, but not limited to two realities

Realism . . . . The philosophy that abstract categories of things, or "universals," are just as real (*res*, "thing") as the particular things in which they are embodied; contrasted with nominalism

OBSCURE CHRISTIAN "ISMS"—CONT.

Sabbatarianism .... The practice of observing the Lord's Day (Sunday) in the manner of the Sabbath day of rest, or of adopting the seventh day (Saturday) as the Christian day of worship and rest

Supralapsarianism .... A form of the doctrine of predestination that holds that God's decrees as to who would be the "elect" occurred before the fall of man; contrasted with infralapsarianism

Ultramontanism .... The tendency in Catholicism to centralize all authority in the pope and the papal *curia*, or Roman congregations (dicasteries or departments)

UNUSUAL ANIMALS OF THE BIBLE

Behemoth (Job 40:15) .... The word *behemoth* is a plural form of the word meaning "cattle." It seems to designate any large animal that lives in marshes. Some interpreters have suggested it refers to the hippopotamus, which means literally in Greek "river horse."

Coney (Prov. 30:26 NIV) .... Also translated "rock badger," the Hebrew word designates an animal about the size of a rabbit that does not burrow but lives in rocky areas. It is not a badger, and some authorities prefer the term *coney*, an old word for "rabbit."

Hoopoe (Lev. 11:19) .... A crested bird with a long, slender bill, with a habit of searching for grubs and insects in manure piles; therefore considered unclean

Kite (Lev. 11:14) .... A scavenger and bird of prey of the hawk family

Leviathan (Job 41:1) .... Used to designate a primeval sea monster defeated by Yahweh (Ps. 74:14); the term in Job seems to refer to any large sea creature, such as a whale.

❈ UNUSUAL ANIMALS OF THE BIBLE—CONT. ❈

Ossifrage (Deut. 14:12 KJV) . . . . . Also translated "vulture," the Hebrew word may designate the lammergeier, or bearded vulture, largest of the vulture family. The term *ossifrage* means "bone-breaker," from the bird's habit of dropping bones or tortoises on rocks to break them.

Phoenix (1 Clement 25–26) . . . . . Not mentioned in the Bible, but in this writing from the *Apostolic Fathers*, the phoenix is a legendary bird that lives five hundred years, then dies. Its "worm" feeds on the carcass of the dead bird, which it embalms and then flies to the altar of the sun in Heliopolis, Egypt. Clement used the phoenix as a symbol of the Resurrection. In the Bible, Phoenix is the name of a harbor town in Crete (Acts 27:12).

Pygarg (Deut. 14:5 KJV) . . . . The King James Version's term for the white-rumped antelope; the Revised Standard Version calls it the "ibex."

Satyr (Isa. 13:21) . . . . In Greek mythology, the satyr is a creature composed of a man and a goat, supposed to inhabit wastelands and ruins. In the Bible, the word seems to refer to demons or is a figurative way of saying that a place will become desolate. Some authorities think it could mean the baboon.

Unicorn (Num. 23:22 KJV) . . . . . . The King James Version's term for the wild ox, probably referring to a species now extinct. The idea of "one horn" is derived from the Greek Old Testament, where a word was used that may have originally designated the rhinoceros.

Water hen (Lev. 11:18) . . . . The meaning of the Hebrew word is uncertain but is thought to refer to one of two hundred species of the rail family that inhabit marshes or ponds. Some authorities think the word refers to an owl.

Talking animals . . . . The serpent in the Garden of Eden spoke with Eve (Gen. 3:1–5). Balaam's donkey carried on a conversation with its master (Num. 22:28–30). The four "living creatures" spoke and sang praise in the Revelation to John.

❧ COMMON ENGLISH PHRASES ❧
TAKEN FROM THE BIBLE

Flesh and bone . . . . Genesis 2:23

Helpmate . . . . Genesis 2:18,
misunderstanding the King James:
"I will make him an help meet [i.e., fitting] for him."

My brother's keeper . . . . Genesis 4:9

Land flowing with milk and honey . . . . Exodus 3:8

An eye for an eye . . . . Leviticus 24:20; Matthew 5:38

The apple of his eye . . . . Deuteronomy 32:10

Rod of iron . . . . Psalm 2:9

My cup runneth over . . . . Psalm 23:5 KJV

No balm in Gilead . . . . Jeremiah 8:22

Handwriting on the wall . . . . Daniel 5:25

The salt of the earth . . . . Matthew 5:13

No one can serve two masters . . . . Matthew 6:24

Straight and narrow . . . . Matthew 7:13–14

Wolf in sheep's clothing . . . . Matthew 7:15

The blind leading the blind . . . . Matthew 15:14

Blood money . . . . Matthew 27:5–6

Physician, heal yourself . . . . Luke 4:23

Eat, drink, and be merry . . . . Luke 12:19

The truth shall make you free . . . . John 8:32

Declared *anathema* . . . . 1 Corinthians 16:22 KJV

Fallen from grace . . . . Galatians 5:4

The root of all evil . . . . 1 Timothy 6:10

SUBJECT INDEX

ACKNOWLEDGMENTS

Apart from my brilliant editor at W Publishing Group, who for some reason asked to remain nameless, there is another whom I would be sorely remiss were I not to thank him from the bottom of my heart: Dr. Richard Leonard. Without Richard none of this would have been possible.